Northeast from Here

Poems by Jeff Coburn

ISBN: 979-8-9933087-0-8

Published by NEKWorks
www.nekworks.com

NEKWORKS

SIMPLE TRUTHS

For those who find wonder in the mundane
and cling, stubbornly, to optimism…

Table of Contents

Part I:
The Roots of Being

Section 1. - The Stillness Between

"The silence is an uncomfortable relief."

Middle Age Lament

Sliding off the bed,
I tap my foot gently on the floor,
testing my knee's memory–
recalling how to bear my weight
before rushing to the bathroom
for my 2 am summons–
all the while lamenting
what age has done to me.

Still, age brings its small rewards:
a deeper respect for silence,
the blessing of warm socks,
and the comfort of knowing
where the ibuprofen is
without switching on the light.

A Proper Cup

A lot can be said
for what goes into a proper cup of tea.

For my mother, the tea must be born
from raging rumbling water,
the kettle screaming its existence to the house.
After boiling, the tea sits, seeps, then cools;
it is sipped warm,
never steaming hot or iced cold,
but it <u>must</u> be produced from boiling water–
no substitutes.

My mother requires simple black tea,
nothing added,
and is known to drink two cups
from the same tea bag.
She uses the same mug the entire day–
by nightfall, tea stains the inside,
encircling it in watercolor rings
of dark and light brown.
Every time I see her cup,
sitting silently on the counter,
waiting for a sip,
I think of love.

My mother was born into a family of tea drinkers.
For my grandmother,
tea was a staple of family gatherings,
along with the weekly collection
of fruit-filled cookies and gossip.
Her daughters gathered around the kitchen table,
greeted with smiles
and steaming cups in flowered patterns.
For her, tea was a welcome home.

My children are fourth-generation tea enthusiasts.
My son scowls when his favorite mug is absent–
he upsets carefully balanced dishes,
seeking to liberate it from the drying rack.
Whatever his mood,
he prefers his tea light brown from cream.
My daughter's tastes are a flight of fancy,
much like her outlook on life:
today it may be watermelon tea,
chilled for two-hours cold brewed–
tomorrow possibly English breakfast
with a hint of maple.
For my kids,
sipping tea is as natural as breathing.

For me, my tastes vary by the hour:
mango ginger in the morning,
cradling the mug like liquid wisdom
as it builds my thoughts
and eases my digestion–
earl grey around midday,
refueling my resolve for the day
with a wake-up caffeine kick–
warm chamomile and honey in the evening,
to loosen my shoulders
and ease me into slumber.

I am proud of my pedigree as a tea drinker,
even if my tastes disagree
with the rest of my family
in terms of what makes a proper cup.

The Warmth Inside

I test my first step–
cautiously toeing slippery winter stairs.
They give a loud crack–
sharp, like a gunshot–
before groaning under my full weight.

Sub-zero weather slams me–
silent yet powerful,
like an unexpected punch to the chest.
I gasp–
my lungs momentarily seize.

My breath settles…
frigid clouds twist above me
with every labored exhale.
The door latches behind,
trapping the waiting warmth inside.

I shuffle to the garage,
legs stiff and unsteady
like a wobbling toy soldier–
frozen ground groans
under my heavy boots.

My hands ache–
stinging, growing pink,
as I fumble for my keys.
If only my fingers were nimble enough
to open the garage while wearing gloves.

The garage door sticks–
an unnoticeable, yet undeniable
frozen warp.
A stubborn standoff begins.

I flinch–
the hairs in my beard
stiffen and stab my face,
joining my raw hands
in its assault against me.

Next door,
warm lights flicker on–
morning rituals begin.
Piping hot decaf will be sipped,
work necessities gathered–
the occupants unaware
(or uncaring)
of the awaiting bitter cold
beyond their comforting home.

I think of my neighbor,
an expectant mother,
standing in her kitchen,
kissing her husband on the cheek,
reminding him to bring his bagged lunch,
hand instinctively clutching her round form–
their awaiting child growing inside.

And I smile,
feeling an unexpected, familiar
warmth inside.

Hum

There is a momentary pop,
Then the world goes silent –
the imperceivable electric hum fades
as the house loses power
just as I rise to make breakfast.

It is New Year's Day–
the world drags itself blurry-eyed
from an evening of champagne bubbles,
lively music, and twinkling new lights–
wondering why the alarm clock is dark,
the coffee didn't start,
and their online tether is cut.

I sit on the edge of the bed,
lamenting the loss of breakfast:
crisp, hickory-smoked bacon,
comforting oolong tea with honey,
crunchy toasty-hot Belgium waffles
dripping with golden Vermont maple,
covered with thawed summer berries
stashed away for a special occasion…

Sighing,
I fumble in the darkness for clothes,
then voyage to inspect the house:
basement breaker hasn't been tripped;
no perceivable trees on the lines;
the neighborhood is dark, as if sleeping,
showing we are not the only ones
sitting alone in the dull morning light.

Last night, the winds howled,
scattering wet snow and icy rain,
as a reminder from Mother Nature
of whom is really in charge this new year.

So, I sit alone in the cold, dark silence,
eating scavenged, leftover fruit
and bottom-of-the box dry cereal,
watching ripples in the puddles outside,
waiting for the hum to return.

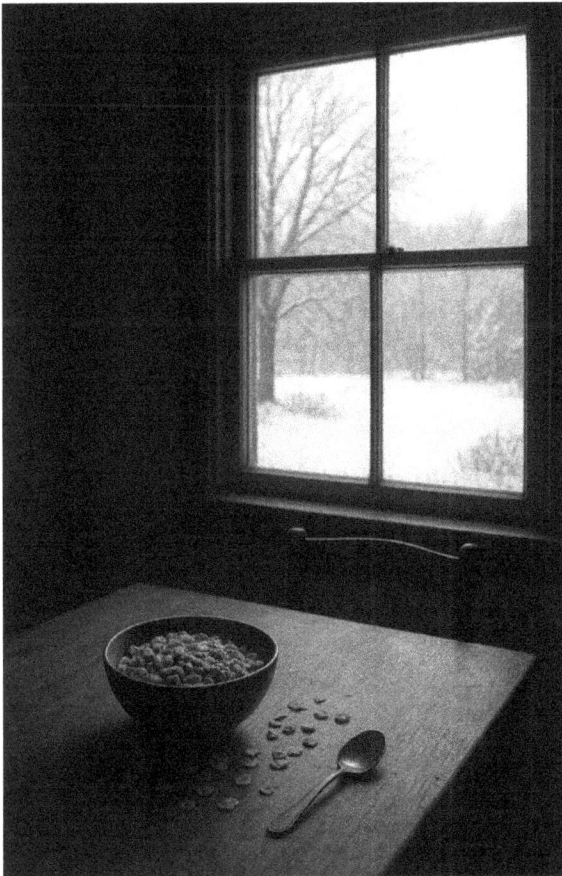

Breathe...

Deep breaths....
Inhale...
Exhale...
Repeat....
Focus on the yoga....
  (Did I remember to turn off the lamp at work?)
Reach up and stretch....
  (I passed by it on my way to filing the report.
  Did I actually turn it off?)
Bend down.....fingers to the floor.

Gentle stretch to the back......
  (Maybe I should call work.....
  maybe the evening custodian will pick up....)
Breathe in. Sun salutation....
  (What's the worst that could happen?
  The boss may get mad....)
Reach to the right....stretch deeply.....
  (....depending on how he liked my report,
  he may already be mad.)
Reach deeper....breath in......
  (Maybe I should run back to work to check?)
Reach to the left....extend your fingers.

Breath out....
  (Traffic is going to be a mess right now.
  Maybe if I go in early tomorrow?)
Breathe in....reach back.....
  (Urgh...can't do that.
  I need to get the twins to daycare.)
Balance on your right foot....
....pull your left one up gently.
  (Wonder when Stu is going in? Maybe he can check.)

Breathe out....
> *(I should just buy one of those Christmas tree timers*
> *to automatically turn off the lamp).*

Tree pose….
> *(If I got a timer, I'd then need to remember*
> *to turn it off on the weekends...)*

Breathe in…..gently lower your leg.
> *(My gosh…I can't believe I'm stressing over a lamp!)*

Balance on your left foot. Breathe in…..
> *(It's that dumb report! Has me in knots!*
> *If I only had more advanced notice...)*

Tree pose on the other side…..
> *(I mean…two days?!? Who sets deadlines like that?)*

Deep breath….

….gently lower down…..

namaste…..
> *(Lamp!)*

Mid-Sunday Spring Nap

Teetering on the precipice
of this world and a dream,
I stir, ever briefly,
at something unseen,
as a late May breeze
tickles at my knee.

It sneaks into my living room,
like a child without a care,
slides through the window,
passes by the chair,
slides around the coffee table,
then gently dances through my hair.

The breeze cradles a chorus:
sweet birdsongs from the trees
blending with children playing,
joyful playground melodies.
The song is half-heard
but still puts me at ease.

My eyelids softly flutter
at the promise of late Spring–
then, the breeze wanders out,
and restlessness settles in.
The echo of the week's trials
linger with me once again.

As my mind gently drifts
for just five more minutes of peace,
the world melts away,
and all my worries cease.
I promise Spring I will return
once I finish my blessed sleep.

first snow

a
single
snowflake
drifts,
dancing
as
it
falls,
a
gift
from
above,
landing
on
my
nose,
disappearing......

except for the smile.

Rare Morning Off

It was a rare morning off–
an unexpected gift
of stillness and simplicity,
free of work and demands–

a moment to sit
idly in my kitchen,
savoring a second cup
of chamomile tea

to inhale the warm scent
of fresh blueberry muffins–
a rare luxury,
I rarely make time for–

a chance to listen
to silence:
the content, steady click
of the kitchen clock,
the soft hum
of the house at rest
almost unnoticeable–

a chance to just.....
be.

But then, the dread returned–

the lure of obligation, creeping in:
an anxious tightness,
seizing my chest,
making it hard to breathe–
an insecure rumble
forming from the back of my mind;
a burning knot
tearing at my stomach.

It is the guilt of enjoying
an unexpected free moment
when there must be SOMEthing
that needs to be done:

ignored spring cleaning,
an impending deadline,
an unorganized sock drawer....
something.

I sigh, low and burdened.

It seems, sometimes,
the hardest thing to do
is nothing at all.

Just a Summer Note

The summer sky melts over the tree line –
    pale ocean blues fading
    into low-hanging clouds,
    drifting like cream-colored foam.
Behind me, a sunset of lemonade pink and yellow
    slips toward slumber,
    silhouetting the band.

Suddenly, the air is alive–

Trumpets blare a reverie,
    rising, climbing,
    hungry to be heard.
The music presses my chest –
    flutes tumble like children,
    wrapped in a blanket
    of clarinet melodies
    and sun-warmed notes.
My head keeps time, nodding and bobbing–
    a subtle, even bounce
    to the thunderous bass drum,
    pulsing behind gleaming trombones,
    shimmering, sliding–
All of it balanced
    upon the venerable presence
    of the park's bandstand.

Soon, the music fades,
    echoing against the hills–
Evening arrives
    with the sinking, slumbering sun
    and the roar of the crowd.

Section 2. – Becoming

"The future, at that time, was a distant country."

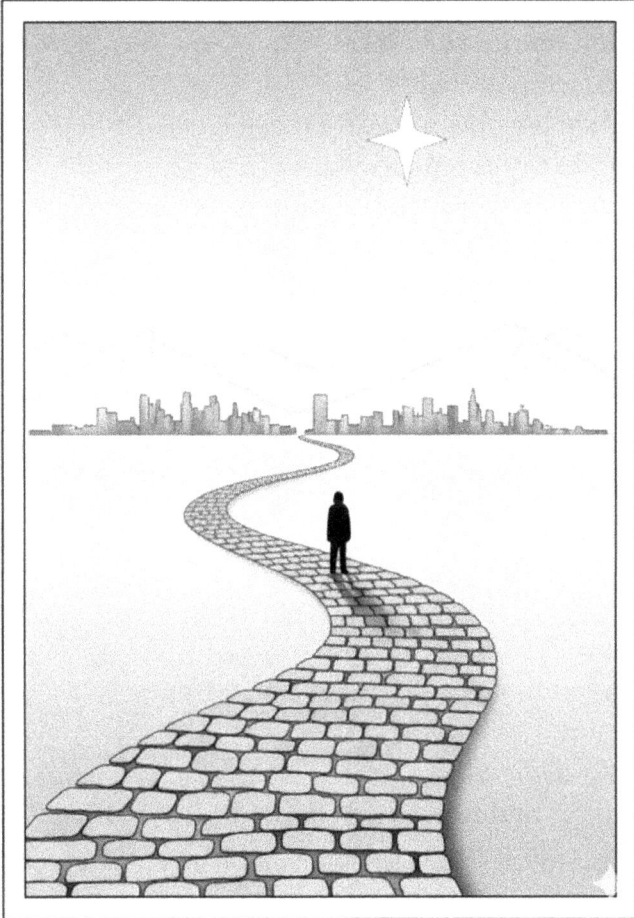

Spring Haircut

The hair tickles my neck
right above the collar.
"Why don't you get a haircut?"
my wife inquires,
glancing at my shaggy mane.

I ignore her momentarily,
munching on my cornflakes
with focused conviction
before they become a mushy mass
dwelling in my cereal bowl.

"I was going to do yard work…"
I respond between bites,
wiping milk from my chin,
glancing over my morning paper
to gauge her reaction.

She gives a slight shrug,
and I know immediately
that I have lost.

For today,
my beloved lawn will remain
a mournful mess
of scattered sticks and sod–
the sopping remains
of a long, cold winter.

Twenty-three minutes later,
I'm on my barber's front stoop.
The striped pole sits motionless–
as if sleeping in
on this lazy Saturday morning.

I squint through the large window,
beyond painted hairdresser scissors
and swooping cursive letters:
"North Street Barber–
A Cut Above the Rest".

Inside, it is dim and still–
missing is the normal commotion:
buzzing electric razors,
sports chatter.
All replaced
by unnatural silence
and an empty barber chair.

Taped to the worn wooden door
is a hand-written sign
proclaiming my fate:
"On vacation - back April 19".

I stare at the sign,
my hair flopping over my ears,
as my lawn beckons my return
12 miles away.

Longing, Belonging

Longing,
to be seen, to exist—
wrapped in the fragile thread of acceptance,
woven into the fabric of every tribe's soul–
to be loved, unconditionally.

Belonging is a primal fire,
flickering in the caves of our ancestors,
whispering through time:
to evolve and thrive, we need another–
to be more than solitary shadows.

But today I am alone. Unmoored.
Adrift, I hear the hum of disconnection,
rattling in the back of my brain like a radiator
fighting the cold of an empty, forgotten room.

My thoughts spiral, a tempest of unheard words,
a scream muffled in an unending void;
I dream of inviting arms, a circle where I matter,
a home that welcomes me, a place that values my
worth.

Then, the winds rise,
carrying a faint, warm whisper:
"Let go, be free —
be wonderfully, amazingly,
uniquely You —
and you will belong."

Four Cats
(a collection of creeping cat haiku)

Cat, Waiting
Patient cat, waiting
for a door to be opened
(due to lacking thumbs).

Sandpaper Kisses
Cool September breeze;
gentle sandpaper kisses.
My special love purrs—

Once a Kitten
Once a small kitten,
zooming down halls, chasing string—
now wise, calm, content.

Midnight Prowl
I stir from my sleep,
aware she is near, unseen—
prowling in the night.

Lessons

Today in school,
I sought to learn what love is.

My English teacher, with a twinkle in his eye,
marked several lines:
    "Tis better to have loved and lost"
        he stated, seemingly lost in a memory,
    "than never to have loved at all,"
        but then he added
    "To thine own self be true".

My music teacher had me listen
to Beethoven and John Lennon,
    pointing out,
        to herself so plainly,
    that love is found in the rise and fall of
crescendos
    and in a chorus that echoes within your soul.

My science teacher charted the stars,
explaining how astrologers mapped love
    through their heavenly path–
    and then,
        with fatherly concern,
    gave me an overview of the reproductive cycle.

My philosophy teacher sighed,
calling love "life's great paradox"–
    explaining theories by
    Aristotle, Nietzsche, and Goethe,
    each one filled with contradictions
        as love often does.

My history teacher spoke about
        Mark Anthony and Cleopatra,
        John and Jackie Kennedy,
        Bonnie and Clyde,
then wiped away a small tear
        at Martin Luther King Jr.'s sacrifice.

My gym teacher fell momentarily silent,
then stated to play for passion, not praise–
        to believe in the value of sacrifice,
        to dedicate yourself to teamwork and trust,
        and to never forget that family
        is more important than a game.

My math teacher smiled and said
that love is an infinite number–
        it cannot be subtracted from,
        is multiplied the more you give,
        and is best when divided by two.

As the day faded, I sat in last period,
absorbing every lesson–

Then, I saw her.

Her eyes caught mine,
her smile greeted mine,
and I realized love's greatest lesson
        is it can never fully be learned.

Annabelle Dreams

1:00 am on Saturday
and Annabelle dreams–
as I shuffle into my home
from a late-night evening
that began early Friday
with a warm cup of tea
to ease my nerves
for whatever trials lay ahead.

I push away work
as Annabelle dreams,
trying to forget
the churning seas
of never-ending tasks
breaking over me.

I itemize my list,
formulating replies,
while shadows stretch
across the coming weekend,
quiet and long,
as Annabelle dreams.

I consider my list
as Annabelle dreams,
time stacked against me
spent on promises kept:
chaperoning 23 high schoolers
for an evening of big city jazz,
on a yellow school bus
filled with energy and sway,
over bumpy spring roads
two hours one way–

But even the lingering song
that eases my soul
can't quiet the clamor
of that persistent list
as Annabelle dreams.

1:30 am, I shuffle to bed,
my work and yellow-bus jazz
still twirling and swirling,
all mixed in my head.
Then I tiptoe into her room
to kiss her on the forehead,
receiving in reply
her still-sleeping smile
as my memories become
part of Annabelle's dreams.

Something Lumbers

7:10 am, and some great beast
stirs upstairs on its way to the bathroom.
I hear it shuffling along heavily,
feet pounding like jackhammers.
  Thump
  Thump
  Thump

Downstairs, the cat pauses–
briefly breaking her morning ritual
of surveying the world
from the dining room window.
  Thump
  Thump
  Thump

She and I exchange worrisome glances,
wondering if the beast
will lumber back to his bed,
task completed,
or come crashing downstairs,
scavenging for breakfast.
  Thump
  Thump
  Thump

I picture him,
scowling at the morning
his lip curled menacingly,
squinting at pale light
peeking, as if frightened,
through the blinds.

He will wander–
somehow both haphazardly and with purpose–
instinct guiding his still-sleeping mind
toward its destined assignment.
     Thump
     Thump
     Thump

His hair will be a
a chaotic tangled mass,
wild and untamed.
His clothing: disheveled–
as if he wrestled his sleepwear
the entire night.
     Thump
     Thump
     Thump

If one dares address him,
the response, if fortunate,
will be a guttural, moaning growl,
rolling from deep in his throat.
If unlucky,
his response will be rapid and biting,
ripping at the morning's peace.
     Thump
     Thump
     Thump

The bathroom door creaks closed…
I hold my breath,
waiting for what comes next…

Then, a fleeting flush of rushing water,
followed by the trickle
of the bathroom sink.
The bathroom door creaks open...
    Thump
    Thump
    Thump

Back to bed he lumbers–
seventeen, and still tired,
while I gather my work,
and my wits,
for the day.

Section 3. – Waning

"The sun can't rise on a broken heart."

Loss Knows No Bias

Loss knows no bias–
It is just as natural to mourn
the loss of your mother–
her image cast like a sorrowful movie
playing in your mind–
as it is to grieve
a lover,
a cat,
a home,
or even your favorite tennis shoes.

Loss is unique–
indescribably different each time.

You can taste it,
sometimes,
like bitter copper
stinging the back of your throat,
or smell it,
like the bite of ammonia in your nose.

You can definitely hear it:
at times shrill and primal,
dragging you into its debilitating pit–
or other times,
an inconvenient grumbling,
planting doubts like bitter weeds.

Still other times,
it slips in softly–
like a whispered song,
providing an unexpected,
therapeutic release.

Sometimes loss helps you grow;
sometimes it just breaks you.

Loss knows no bias
because eventually,
it chooses us all.

Symmetry

"Tyger, tyger, burning bright...."
        As a child, I met perpetual fright–
        Head under the covers every night.
        I would lie awake, fearing the dark unknown
        Listening to the terror I seemed to own.

        My dreams rumbled with monstrous groans,
        Twilight shrieks that chilled my bones,
        Leaving my soul fragile and slight–
        Swallowed whole by the fearful night.

        In the morning, my mother hid her face
        As I buried my own disgrace
        In a bowl of colorless, tepid oatmeal–
        A contrast to her eye, shining silver-blue steel.

        As I grew, my courage began to grow
        As I discovered poets like Hughes and Poe;
        Slowly I began to uncover my head
        From the flashlight's glow, reading in my bed.

        Before I left for college one early autumn eve,
        My sister crept to my room, grasping my sleeve.
        Clutching me, sobbing, eyes filled with tears–
        Lip quivering, body trembling, sharing her
        fears–

        She told me how our stepdad just beat her.
        Between her cries, my mind started to blur;
        Images of our mom watching in silence
        As her daughter's life crumbled to violence.

My sister sat there, without a word–
My mind was shattered, truth turned absurd,
As slowly…painfully….it all took shape
As my sister whispered details of the rape.

Thinking back to when I was young,
All my false monsters became undone.
As reality crept in, I understood why I hid
                (burying my head
                hiding in poetry lines
                blocking the pain
                with silent designs)
From the true horrors my stepdad did.

I rose, gently patting my sister on her shoulder
With my eyes tearing hot, starting to smolder–
I reached next to my bed for my baseball bat,
Paused once more, giving my sister a final pat.
As slowly the lines of a poem came to me...
I found myself saying,
"What fearful symmetry."

Upon Her, Passing

How do you measure unwanted silence?

Is it motionless disbelief,
your expression confused, transfixed?
Or is it endless, echoing seconds–
long, uneasy, laboring ticks?

Is it sacred quiet moments spoiled,
turned lonely, worn, and tainted?
Or is it strangers, waiting in sterile rooms,
barely acquainted, bound by discomfort?

Perhaps it is not quiet at all,
but breath released,
then held fast,
deep and tight?

Or maybe it is sanity
taking flight?

The Waning Hour

"Are you getting up?" she asks, uncertain,
curious of the late morning hour.
I bury my head under my pillow.

".....no," I reply, distantly, considering–
I have given up the day
before it has even begun.

Instead, I embrace the wonderful bitterness of defeat,
leaning into my depression,
letting go of hope–
no longer grasping
at my self-indulgent stubbornness
like a life raft
keeping my tired sense of self-worth afloat.

I fear death–
the pain, the pointless uncertainty–
but I also fear life:
left as a hollow echo,
wishing to no longer exist,
clinging to the invisible tether
of her concerned, wayward glance–

stuck in the quiet, in-between moments
of the waning hour.

Yet, I rise—
for her, to ease her concern,
to wear the illusion of strength
for the one who still believes.

First Fall

The fall came early–
winter came earlier still.
The days grew short and grey;
my optimism faded in the waning light.

I slipped one morning, leaving for work.
Fighting a nagging, pervasive sickness–
acidic bile eating my stomach–
my body gave out under its own weight.

I laid there on unforgiving concrete,
icy cold needles stabbing my lungs,
the familiar copper taste on my tongue–
paralyzed, fearful to move on.

Not sure what else to do,
I prayed–
pleading for the light to return,
begging for healing warmth.

The Windowless Room

I sit in the windowless room;
The world beyond me is timeless.
The event is not quite crimeless;
I am robbed of autumn's plume.

Outside, cascading fall leaves bloom,
Brilliant colors mark the climates.
I sit in the windowless room;
The world beyond me is timeless.

I trade the colors for drab gloom;
Gray walls trapping me in silence
As I fight an autumn virus.
Trapped here alone–my sickbed tomb.
I sit in the windowless room.

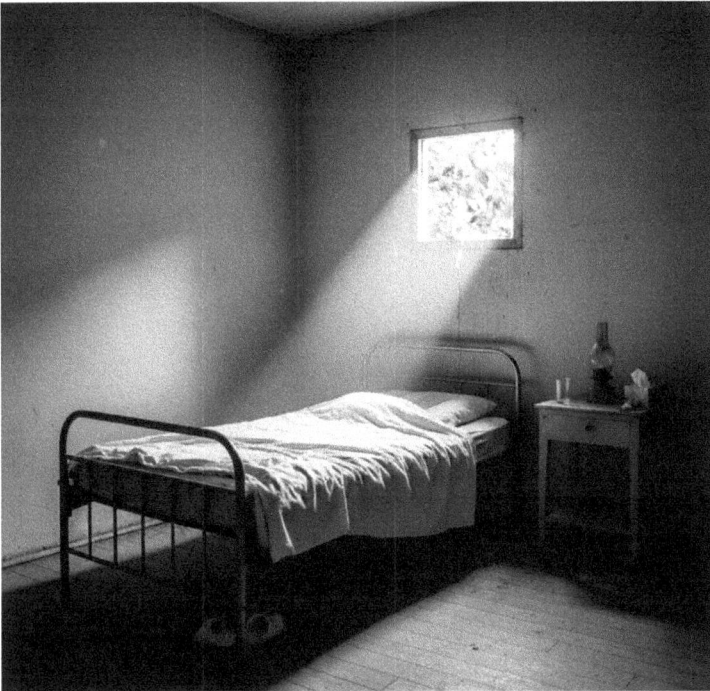

A Momentary Loss

My wife leans through the door
this sunlit, early Sunday morning,
having momentarily lost me.

She finds me at my desk,
gazing out the window,
trying to pen the world to paper.

She sighs–relieved just to see me,
and smiles softly my way.
"Good...you're okay..."

I feel her twisting panic slip away,
like morning dew, retreating from the sun–
she found what she had lost.

She slips back
to her morning rituals,
and I realize:

the world's true miracles
are not in exotic lands
or marvels of art–

they live in the quiet search
of a wonderful woman
seeking her love
on a too-quiet morning
just to know
that I'm okay.

Stories Left Behind

Everyone has a story:

An embellished tale of valor,
shared over uproarious raised pints
in the fellowship of a dimly-lit pub;

A beloved memory of winters past,
cuddling under heavy, warm quilts,
watching a ballet of tumbling snow;

The road trip to discover oneself
among roadside oddities
and conversations in small-town diners;

The year battling against cancer,
not dwelling on the persistent nausea,
but instead savoring the small moments.

Life is full of unknown twists and turns,
each journey is worth its quiet rewards–
they are testaments that we exist.

How a story is ultimately judged
is not on fanfare or enormity,
but in how it lingers–
how it enriches
those who remain.

Dusk

A hint of relief creeps forward,
on this stifling summer evening,
painting the world a fleeting pink
beneath streaked cotton candy clouds.
I sit on the porch, lips too dry to even whisper,
as the day melts and sighs–
seeking release from the relentless heat.

Dusk descends,
folding vibrant pink clouds
under a calm blanket of soulful indigo.
Silhouetted trees fade,
their leaves, deep greens and whispered blacks,
layered like memories on their branches.
A streetlamp flickers awake,
humming to the approaching night,
waiting for freedom from the heat.

Inside, the cat cries for me,
awakened by darkness, and suddenly alone.
She found refuge from the heat,
curled somewhere beneath the couch,
but has now emerged,
abandoned.

My stomach tightens, twists, and sinks–
while I envied her escape,
I would rather bear intolerable heat
then wake to the voiceless twilight,
and feel—even for a moment—
that everyone who loves me
had quietly, without warning,
disappeared.

Part II:
The World in Focus

Section 4. – Field Notes

"The ocean whispers truths I am still learning."

Sap Run

March arrives with a hint of joy:
warming afternoons for the sun to enjoy,
bringing with it freely flowing sap –
trees waking from their annual nap.

Winter retreats from open hills
seeking refuge in lingering chills –
forest snow, still a foot deep
holds the trees in an icy keep.

It's 1960—a new decade stirs.
The tractor bounces, then sputters and purrs.
Forgotten paths fill with youthful noise
carrying a band of middle-school boys.

The tractor halts; the kids deploy–
gathering buckets with scurrying joy,
wading into the thigh-high snow
all for the promise of maple-glazed dough.

The sap settles and boils; hours pass, unaware –
slow alchemy in copper, brewed with patient care.
At last, the boys receive their hard-earned prize:
warm donuts with syrup, joy wide in their eyes.

Barefoot Days

Rising solstice, endless days –
June brings bright mornings full of promise,
afternoons warm like wildflower honey.
Calm evenings on the porch refresh our souls,
renewed since spring rains and winter naps.

Barefoot, carefree summer days –
July blooms with light yellow sunflower dresses;
toes kiss freshly cut grass
as mornings run into evenings,
drifting into gentle waves of warm smiles.

Evenings cool, gardens bloom –
August mornings glisten with dew;
days shorten, evenings creep earlier,
summer lingers, tired yet full of conviction,
cradling waning warmth like sunshine gold.

Leaves hint at the promise of color –
September arrives, warmth fading to soft light;
the Fair is gone, wooden horses rest,
children again rush home from school.
Autumn peeks around the corner, looking to arrive.

Creeping vines, pumpkins content and fat –
October's autumn trees ignite and bloom;
balmy afternoons sigh for a final time,
sunshine moments spent raking vibrant hues.
Summer days slip quietly away–
replaced again with evening snuggling blankets.

Dew Glistens

Cool September, Saturday morning –
a gently rolling sea of grass:
  dark primal emerald,
  peppy bright lime,
  content forest green.
Dew glistens, each droplet sparkling
  like a canopy of pinpoint midnight stars.
A wondrous tapestry is woven for me,
  the gift of a rare moment
  somehow vivid yet tranquil.
I linger, contemplating, then decide:
it is too damp to mow –
  a labor for after the sun rises.

Fall   Leaves

Leaves
    Leap,
        Tumble
Turn,
          Twisting and
    Dancing,
Spinning
     and
        Swirling–
a kaleidoscope
    of Early
Autumn
     October colors–
        Living yellows,
    Moving reds,
Breathing oranges–
      Mixed with
         Falling greens
    of Summer's
fading
       promises–
Prancing about
         as if caught
    in a twister
Only
    Two
      Feet
        High–
    Rising
     and Falling,
Swiveling
    About
      until
    the Wind
     Suddenly
      Dies
   and they
     all
     just
      Fall

Black Winter Cat

Curled up in her box,
lined with woolen hats and worn socks,
the cat soaks up rare February warmth;
sunlight peeks through the mudroom windows,
a momentary respite from winter snows.

She snores serenely and lightly,
with her chest rising slightly,
a mound of black fur content in her slumber–
she relishes the precious hours of sun
before winter's evening's chill comes.

An hour later, as I relax in my chair,
the cat wanders by absently, without a care;
she enters the room, stretches and yawns,
then leaps upon me to continue her nap,
her sunshine departed, settling for my lap.

Tending Lines

Driving down a snow-scattered back road,
once covered in summer dust and dirt,
I see my neighbor tending his tap lines.

I slow, as if he won't notice me—
as though he might wander into the road
like some newborn fawn.

In truth, he's too absorbed in his pipeline
to stray into harm's way.
I consider stopping to help,
then wonder what I know about sugaring
that would provide any sort of relief.

Deciding the value is in the offer,
not the know-how,
I ease into a safe alcove,
safe from any unlikely traffic
on this late February afternoon.

I remember long-past days–
My father driving his old Buick
down these same Vermont roads.

Back then, maple trees wore
crooked, dented sap-buckets–
not vacuum-pressured plastic tubes,
hanging like Christmas garlands
along the trunks.

Suddenly, I wish Dad were here with me,
in his old tan deerskin gloves
and flannel hunting jacket,
offering to help a neighbor
we barely know
tend his lines.

Dad has been gone almost 17 years–
yet, somehow,
he is still with me
as I give my neighbor a friendly wave.

Rhubarb Crane

"There's a crane!" (I exclaim)
"in the rhubarb patch today!
It's standing, quite demanding
for an audience to come stare!
Perched motionless, so grand,
where it can be seen by all of us!
Come look!"

I hear a crash, then in a dash,
my wife, in a tizzy, almost dizzy,
rushes in, with an optimistic grin,
and a trail of scattered, forgotten linen
left in a lurch, dropped and dangling,
the source of the thunderous thud.
"Look!" (I exclaim).

She squints, and she scowls.
"You ninny..." she groans,
"that isn't a bird,
you squat little turd,
but instead only a twisted, turned leaf!"

My nose twists, causing her fits,
as well as an audible moan;
"see there, you buffoonish old bear!
It isn't so rare for you to be unaware
that your facts are in complete disarray–"

"See here!" (she yells quite clear)
"that thing you think is a beak
is just a slight tweak
of twisted rhubarb leaf,
and the feet
are only its stalk!"

I shrug, slightly worried,
as she, most assuredly,
begins to steam with heat
from a fury and frustration and hurrying.

She rolls her wide eyes,
throwing her hands to the skies–
then, barely beginning,
storms staunchly out,
giving me a shout
while throwing stray socks about,
and tossing me a toppled pile
of lopsided linen:

She declares with audible heat
as she makes her retreat,
"if you want to play birdwatcher, fine—
but you can refold the sheets."

The Deer of Cumberland

The day after Thanksgiving,
I set out to walk off my lunch–
a leftover turkey sandwich,
served cold,
with homemade buffalo mayo,
onions, and baby spinach–
just how I like it.

We're in Rhode Island, visiting family.
While others venture into glorious battle
in the retail frenzy known as "Black Friday",
I strike out for the bike path in Cumberland–
a quiet stretch of woods
tucked away like a forgotten memory,
here in the city.

Passing tall November trees,
entering leafless winter slumber,
I feel the call from home–
back to rolling Vermont hills,
already hushed by snow–
far from the commotion
of traffic and shopping malls.

I casually nod and greet those I pass.
Some ignore me,
others return a cautious hello.
I am an anomaly,
a stranger making a casual acquaintance.

Crossing a wooden bridge
stretching across a marshy bog,
I count each slat as though it matters.
The woods feel like a lifelong friend–
more comforting than apprehensive strangers
who suspiciously pass me by.

Nearing the end of the path, I pause–

I sense it before any real indication:
an odd calmness,
like the world holding its breath…
familiar, invisible eyes
watching me from the maze of barren trees.

I stop, unmoving, held fast like stone–
staring into the woods,
keeping my breath tight and short,
fearing any movement
will startle my unseen companion.

I burrow my glance into the woods–
after eternally long moments
I see eyes staring back:
dark, shimmering,
like calm midnight pools .

I make out the long, pointed snout,
then see the subtle twitch of the ears.
It is a doe, barely a season old,
seemingly as surprised that I noticed her
as I was to find a rare piece of home.

My eyes shift–
I make out another head behind her,
maybe 10 feet deeper into the woods.
Soon, I notice the third,
hidden in a deep, tangled thicket
only 15 feet away.

I stand, quietly–
a walker passes,
giving me an odd glance,
not seeing what I have to share.
She is lost in her earbuds
and misses the mysterious wonder
of what could have been.

The sky blooms purple and pink,
as the deer creep out—six in all:
two bucks, one with small nubs,
the other a proud four-point crown,
flanked by three healthy doe,
and a hesitant fawn
(wisely unsure of my presence).

They graze on crabapples and thistle.
I stay, watching my friends enjoy their buffet–
time forgets to move.

Eventually, I turn back,
deciding to leave before nightfall,
zipping my coat higher,
feeling the chill settle in.
Thankful for finding
an unexpected piece of home
hidden in the city
along this stretch of woods.

Icy Summer Sting

Aching icy summer heat,
sipping chilled water
over frozen cubes–
fleeting sharp throbbing teeth.

Sunshine scorching,
torrid, unrelenting,
makes this cold relief
worth the temporary stings.

Thaw

Descending the cellar stairs,
I meet the cold breath of concrete–
damp, musty, and unsettling.

I step off with a light splash,
water rippling around me,
as I wade carefully into
a six-inch deep lagoon–
reality sinks in.

The winter thaw has come.
Water creeps through every crevice,
quietly rising from unnoticeable fissures
in the concrete floor.
The groundwater is so high
that it bubbles up, not down.

Shuffling forward,
an oddly refreshing coolness
momentarily strikes–
I wonder if my rubber boots leaked
before determining
it is just winter's final gasp.

A trio of beach coolers float lazily by,
like boats on some still ocean;
I pluck them from the water,
like happy bobbing children
waterlogged from a day at the beach,
and place them with care
on the refuge of dry cellar stairs.

Remnants of insulation
float below the basement tides,
hanging like thick, submerged blankets–
reclaiming them, if possible,
will be a task to tackle another day.

The basement dims as I go,
its windows still covered
to stand against the winter cold–
their corners are painted
with now-forgotten cobwebs.

At last, I arrive at the pump,
its automatic bobber stuck
as if too lazy to move.
I give it a gentle kick,
bumping the switch into place,
and the pump stirs to life
with a rhythmic, purring hum.

I stare at the pump,
grasping its corrugated piping,
feeling rushing water depart.
Standing there, waiting,
I suddenly feel irony's sting–

Recalling how hard I prayed
for winter's chill to finally fade,
never considering
what it might leave behind.

A Stone by the Sea

"What are you doing?"
she asks, as I stare at the ground.

My eyes trace the stone's craggy lines,
shaped by years of restless tides.
Slabs of granite, basalt, and quartzite
fit together like an imperfect jigsaw—
a natural dike stretching its arms to the sea,
welcoming like an expectant lover.

I'm transfixed by the tumble of browns and grays,
separate yet entwined,
an earthen, living marriage.

Without looking up, I answer:
"I'm contemplating the existence of this rock."

She's quiet,
trying to gauge whether I'm serious
or just setting the stage for another whim.
Her expression says it all—
she's been here before.
"...why?"

I breathe in deep–
the ocean air fills me,
with the subtle familiarity
of a long-lost friend.

"I wonder…"I begin,
"how many have passed this stone–
their hearts full of hope
or heavy with grief?

How many have sat here,
watching the rolling grey sea,
embraced in awe, fear, or peace?

Did someone walk here,
hand in hand with a pregnant wife,
heart thudding with joy?
Or come to forget–
to bury the ache of a lost love?

How many children leapt across the stone
as if it were a giant toadstool?
How many wishes fell upon it,
like flakes of Christmas snow?

How many storms has it weathered?
How many sunlit days has it seen?
And how many of those days
mirrored the souls of those who passed by?"

She sighs—
long and knowing–yet patient.
Taking my hand,
her half-playful smile breaks the quiet.
"Come on, Emily Dickinson," she calls.
"There are plenty more stones to see."

The Last Day of May

It is the last day of May.
Unseasonably, uncomfortably cold,
Beneath a solemn overcast sky,
Heavy wet and gray.

It is Memorial Day.
No marching bands or grand parade–
Only a line of umbrellas
Protecting against the chilling rain.

For the honored, fallen dead,
Only a simple crowd of nine.
For those we lost on distant shores
A mourning mother bows her head.

Far from home, another dies;
Tears shed, bleeding blue and red,
Over ideals greater than some hill.
A cardinal flies –

After the service, no one stays.
Puddles form, comradery strays,
The gathered sullenly shuffle away
On these final moments of May.

Section 5. – Urban Beats, Rural Rhythms

"Alone like a ship adrift on cold seas."

Yesterday's Takeout

Four months into quarantine–
the car reeks like curbside pizza,
pepperoni and oregano
hanging in the air
like Chef Boyaredee
was stitched in the upholstery.

The gas gauge hovers
a little under three-quarters of a tank–
I try to recall when I last filled up,
relenting to the vague recollection
"last month…or so".

Most of my days
now have the qualifier "or so".
I struggle to tell Mondays from Thursdays;
weeks blend like half-mixed paint–
spirals that don't start or end.

I strain to recall the life before–
friends huddled around the bar table
sharing drinks and stories
over half-off appetizers,
our laughter joined
by the buzz of the crowd.
Those days seem so long ago–

Now all that remains
is the unsettling hush
of the idle car
and the lingering ghost
of yesterday's takeout.

Lost Hour, Fallen Snow

It's dreaded Monday, day one of the grind–
the glorious weekend is completely behind,
leaving drowsy eyes, desperate for rest.

It's 6 am; I am robbed of needed sleep–
daylight savings arrived, an annual thief.
I'm left sipping wearily on caffeinated tea.

Last night, under darkness, crept in the snow,
slipping into town, wherever it could blow,
arriving like an unexpected, unwanted house guest.

Outside, my neighbor battles wet snow,
parting huge piles wherever he goes,
alone like a ship adrift on cold seas

Even though there is no service today,
he commits his labors, while my energy strays,
as if this vacant church were the only place to go.

As his shovel scrapes against worn concrete,
I wonder whether it's obligation or conceit
that drives my neighbor to clear morning snow.

Shopper's Funk

Eyes glazed, senses dazed,
lulled by overhead flickering fluorescents
and an endless loop of '80s synth-pop
playing over and over and over –
piping through tinny ceiling speakers
suspended above steel-grey metal racks
filled with overpriced beige chinos
and pastel polos with stiff collars.

This is my personal purgatory:
enduring the shopper's funk
while also dreading
the next credit card statement.

Next to me, a kinship forms
with another tortured soul–
a preschooler, mid-meltdown,
cycling through the stages
of shopping fatigue:
hungry, thirsty, tired, bored.

His mother, unfazed,
debates between a garish
pink and yellow flower-print shirt
or diaper-brown corduroy overalls
plucked from the bargain rack.

"Just 10 more minutes...."
My wife drones on, absently,
for the third (or fourth?) time
in the last half hour.
I fight a yawn, my jaw seizing,
as dignity fades behind bleary eyes.

Weekend shopping is a circle of hell,
redeemed only by
food court funnel cake
and the gleam in my wife's eye
as she unearths some hidden treasure
like an archaeologist
discovering the Sphinx
beneath clearance tags.

This is love:
sacrificing your sanity
for the momentary spark
of someone else's joy.

Borderline

Urban legends cling to the Haskell–
a 400-seat opera house
with near-perfect sight lines
and unique ambiophonic sound–
the space breathes in stereo.

It straddles an invisible seam:
Derby Line in Vermont,
Stanstead in Quebec.
A faded black line bisects the floor.
Sit where you like–
but leave as you entered,
to ensure the border "stays intact".

Some say it's haunted:
cold shivers that linger,
soft knocks and dragging backstage.
One legend claims Samuel Insull–
innovator, investor, disgraced electric mogul–
built it for his mistress,
whose voice cracked more than it soared.
They call it "the Citizen Kane Connection,"
a mirror for the movie's plot.

But the story most whispered
is the one that echoes deepest–
they say the Beatles once practiced here.
A secret reunion of legends,
a flash of impossible harmony,
a gathering of wayward friends.
George and John on the Canadian side
(barred from U.S. soil),
Paul and Ringo across the aisle,
separated only by a line on the floor–
an imaginary boundary.

It was a small, secret act of defiance,
screamed through guitar riffs and drumrolls.
They were unwanted immigrants,
rebels–
putting aside differences,
healing old wounds
in whispered harmonies–
an act of shared joy
and borderless dissent.
Customs never caught the chorus.

True or not–
that's yours to decide.
This is the Haskell's lasting gift:
not just the performances
that grace this borderless place,
but the legends that set the stage
and hold the line.

Life Imitating Life

the air handler kicks in,
a low, rhythmic throbbing–
(whir, whir, whir)–
felt in my head
as much as heard.

artificially cool air,
flows overhead–
like some languid stream
dancing across my hair,
rippling, unseen.

sweat beads beneath my bottle,
reflecting fluorescent glare–
a glinting pulse,
like an indifferent,
electric god.

my stomach twists–
this place is me:
perpetually stuck,
living a false life,
moving nowhere.

bright summer light
peeks through distant windows,
whispering seductively–
reminding me there is existence
beyond this lifeless room

the light speaks of a place
where trees tilt in warm breezes,
and the air tastes real–
an elsewhere beyond
the artificial hum.

and suddenly, I long for more:
something greater
than the daily monotony–
the freon-cooled hiss
of life imitating life.

Washed Up

How is it that people can use public restrooms
and not wash their hands?
Is their time so valuable
that they can't spare 60 seconds
to wash, scrub, rinse, (repeat, please,) and dry?

Are they uncomfortable with
public displays of cleanliness?
Do they think they are impervious
to accidentally splattered transient germs,
like some kind of "anti-icky" forcefield
is activated when they approach the commode?

Do they believe that urinals
are magical porcelain fountains
in sacred public shrines,
and that washing after tinkling
is tainting that holy experience?

Are they time-travelers from some far-off future
where invisible energy waves
sanitize people from head to toe
every time they exit a restroom?

I ponder the enormity of all this
as I contemplate how to safely open
the men's room door–
the crooked bronze handle
seeming to taunt me,
daring me to grasp it,
as I realize there are no paper towels
anywhere in sight....

Clips

My son waits in the kitchen
        sitting on a well-worn wooden stool
        more often used to fetch high bowls
        or as a perch for our waiting cat
            (queen of our house)
        than to sit.

His thumb scrolls through his phone,
        dodging the latest political headline
        (criticisms of how "the other party"
        is mismanaging the latest crisis),
        pausing instead at a video montage
        of a lucha libre wrestler's greatest moves.

He sits there, dutifully, as his mother and girlfriend
discuss hair ties:
        reviewing a variety of clips and clasps,
        detailing where they originated,
        discussing their practical and fashionable uses,
        clarifying the best type of hair for each.

He sits there, patiently, unintrusive,
        quietly waiting for them to finish,
        surrounded by a language he doesn't
understand,
        while watching Rey Mysterio
        soar across his phone.

Vampire Weekend

Two hours early–
an 81-degree warming sun
after an unseasonably damp spring.
About ninety minutes from home–
waiting.

Far across the fairgrounds,
metal scaffolding, shrouded in black,
rises above swaying summer trees.
The band rehearses–
the concert before the concert.

Guitars hum familiar chords,
echoing against the bandstand;
a percussion rhythm rises.
A voice calls–
"There was someone just like me…"

The parking lot attendant stiffens–
he nervously eyes an oncoming RV
sporting an airbrushed desert scene:
faded yellow sunsets
over rolling brown sands.

Soon, the drums pound a primal growl–
the guitar momentarily weeps.
Vampire Weekend plays.
But the parking attendant is oblivious
to all but his already crooked line.

Demarcus Cousins
(aka "Boogie 2018")

I read the news that Demarcus "Boogie" Cousins
signed with a new team:
Rattlesnake, Wildcat, King, Pelican,
Warrior–

People claim Cousins is planning on riding on coattails
to be a champion–
bandwagon, turncoat, opportunist, villain,
person–

People say he is a loose cannon–
suspended, fined, dirty, fighter,
passionate–

People say a lot about Demarcus Cousins,
but do they always tell the entire story?
Hostile, unprofessional, disruptive, selfish;
scorer, rebounder, all-star, Olympian;
player, son, father, man,
human–

Life is complex–
so are people,
probably including
Demarcus Cousins.

Section 6. – A Wry Glance

"Expecting a symphony, receiving a song."

If I Were a Duck

If I were a duck
and you were a pond,
I would float there forever–
>   (now that sounds all wrong…)

If you were a paper
and I was some glue,
I would stick to you forever–
>   (now that just won't do!)

If I were a guitarist
and you were a pick,
I would pluck you forever–
>   (I think I'm going to be sick…)

If you were Saran Wrap
and I were a dish,
you'd cling to me forever–
>   (yeah right…I wish…)

If I were a dog
and you were the yard,
I'd claim you forever–
>   (why is poetry so hard?)

If I were your husband
and you were my wife,
we'd love one another forever–
>   for the rest of our life.

Witch What

A witch named What was in a rut–
her brews waned into watery stews.
What wondered what weakened her potions
into lesser, pathetic, non-potent brews.

Was it poorly poured witch hazel?
Or needlessly knotty newt eyes?
Did her sister Who, who visited at noon,
swap her goop for goulash soup?

What wondered and wandered,
her thoughts all askew,
waxing wearily on forgotten witchy ways,
and her possibly corrupted cauldron
that smelled suspiciously of stew.

She paced, prodded, stirred, and sputtered,
until, at a standstill,
What once again sampled
her broken witch brew.

She stopped, pondered, puckered–
then What sighed…
rolled her witchy wide eyes,
smacked her witchy limp lips,
and resigned to remain What,
the witch of tasty stew.

Leroy's Socks

Leroy's socks are blue today–
they were never intended to be that way,
but the washing machine had its say…
so Leroy's socks are blue today.

Leroy's socks are a mix of hues,
all of which are shades of blues:
cobalt, cyan, and even aqua-chartreuse….
Leroy's socks are a symphony of blues.

Leroy's socks were once white,
but now they're quite a curious sight.
His mother warned "don't mix dark and light!"
But he ignored her and caused this plight.

But Leroy likes his socks just fine.
For him, the "disaster" turned out sublime!
Perhaps his laundry could be a sign,
that it's wonderful to be unique and shine–
to let your colors mix and combine.

The Love of Dry Toast

I woke this morning in a tizzy–
excited, but also mixed with dread;
tasked with a creative masterpiece,
I drafted the menu in my head.

We'd start with a golden omelet,
with mushrooms, kale, and brie,
then cinnamon French toast piled high
with maple, strawberries, and cream.

The bacon would be crisp and smoky,
the oranges would be freshly squeezed–
when you saw the grand buffet,
you'd nearly buckle at the knees.

Alas, I dropped all the eggs
and never got the kale.
When I discovered I had lost the bacon,
I knew my masterpiece would surely fail.

So instead, this morning, I served dry toast,
with juice straight from a can,
and one recovered fried egg on the side,
which, of course, promptly ran.

I guess it was the thought that counts,
so now all that I can say,
is "enjoy your dry toast masterpiece...
oh, and Happy Mother's Day!"

Grapefruit

Time stops –
Life momentarily suspended
like a forgotten flower in warm amber.

I catch my first glimpse of her:
straight, shoulder-length hair
jet black like a tranquil night,
pinned back with turquoise-blue clips
that sport sea turtles;
soft, calm eyes,
with just the slightest hint of playful trouble;
and a thin, unassuming smile,
captivating yet simple,
like a modern-day Mona Lisa.

I instinctively hold my breath–
my heart pounds in my ears.

Such is my downfall.
I crash into the supermarket's fruit display,
my mind absorbed only on her.
Grapefruits tumble to the floor,
scattering like excited wayward children.

I stand there, embarrassed and dumbfounded,
until I hear a slight laugh.
"Don't worry," she says,
"Last week I knocked over the coconuts."
And so, a little spark grows
in a special shared moment
while in the produce aisle.

Bench Verse

I sit on the bench,
foot tapping uneven cobblestones,
while my love strolls the courtyard,
browsing boutique windows.

My pencil in hand,
I pass time crafting limericks–
self-amusing anecdotes
on those who pass by:

> *Mr. and Mrs. were up all night*
> *Yelling and screaming: a horrible fight!*
> *But from what I am told,*
> *Is that once you're consoled,*
> *The "making up" justifies the battle quite right.*

Noting a nearby labradoodle,
I commence to write:

> *A dog's love for his owner is grand;*
> *In truth, the two of us go hand-in-hand.*
> *But a cold lick to my nose*
> *Is not as good, I suppose,*
> *As whatever these two lovebirds have planned.*

Noticing one absent wedding ring,
I continue:

> *My neighbor loves to mock me all day;*
> *"You're bookish and boorish!" is what he will say.*
> *But on his behalf,*
> *I will have the last laugh,*
> *When his wife hears who he was hugging today.*

Then I catch sight of my love–
in her new yellow dress,
bright, yet outshone by her smile.

And just like that,
all my little stories fade away
in the joy of her.

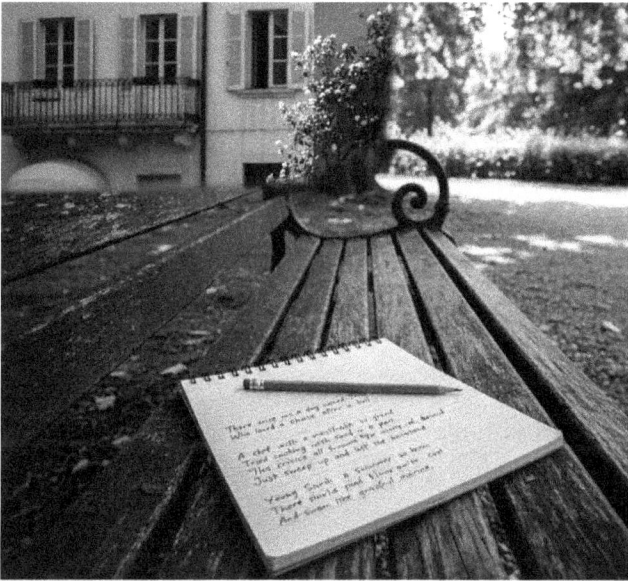

Man's Best F(r)iend

Some like them furry–
      (cue sniffling, red-eyed allergies)
Some like them to slither–
      (like cold chills up my back)
Some like them tiny–
      (aren't gerbils just rats with good PR?)
Some like them to swim–
      (but don't they just float there?)
Some like them in cages–
      (jailed instead of in the sky)
Some like them with eight legs–
      (screaming "get it off! get it off!!")
Some like them for walking–
      (scoop the poo off my lawn)
Some like them to fetch sticks–
      (where is the dignity in that?)
Some like them as companions–
      (cats own you–you don't own them)
Some like them to chase toy mice–
      (secret plot to lull you into submission, human...)
Some like them to ride on–
      (so, you smell like manure?)
Some like them to moo–
      (you smell even worse....)
Some like them for their eggs–
      (that's what grocery stores are for)
Some like them exotic–
      (flamboyant "look at me!" types)
Some like them in droves–
      (crazy cat woman–or dog guy–or goat herder...)
Me? I value what matters:
Quiet. Loyal. Emotionally stable.
I like pet rocks.

Popcorn Bits

I thought myself clever
flipping the popcorn bag upside down,
opening it from the bottom,
certain that my sister
would then be stuck
with all the broken bits
and teeth-cracking kernels
lingering at the bottom of the bag.

To my dismay,
as soon as I turned the bag over,
all the kernels fell to the top.

Such is life:
no matter how much you twist it,
all the unsavory bits
still need to be addressed
in the end.

Rondal Prime

I just Googled "poetry types",
As my brain was stuck on a rhyme.
I stumbled on "rondal" in time
And gave those pages idle swipes.

"Thirteen lines, three stanzas" it hypes
With eight syllables in each line.
I just Googled "poetry types",
As my brain was stuck on a rhyme.

But you can stray from archetypes
For you can add an extra line!
In fact, "rondel prime" sounds sublime....
But "no poetry skills" (he gripes).
I just Googled "poetry types"
As my brain was stuck on a rhyme.

Part III:
The Journey

Section 7. – Two

"The beauty is in the joining, not the perfection."

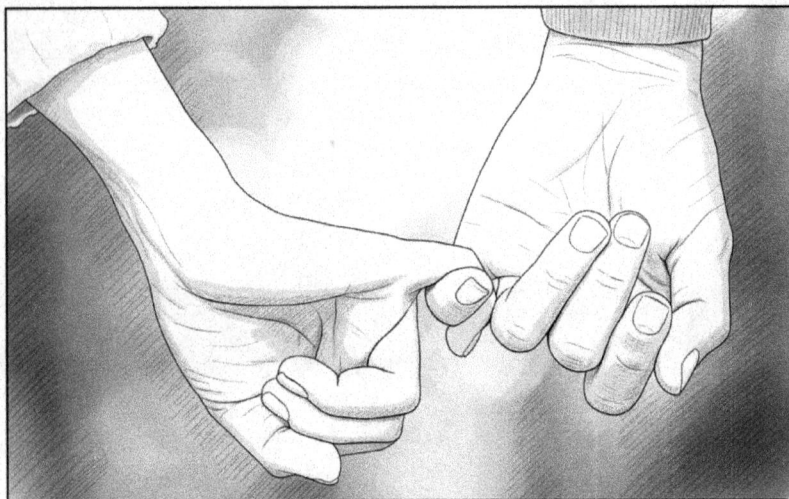

Five More Minutes

The rain pitter-pats
Like dancing cats
On the metal porch roof
Outside her bedroom window.

Her eyelids flutter
And her fingertips shudder
As she motions me away.
"Just....five more....minutes...."

Downstairs the coffee brews
Bringing courage anew
In the form of a caffeine kick
awaiting to start her day.

I linger and smile,
Glancing at her a while,
Until she stirs and turns,
then mumbles: "Fine…"

Her hair is a mess,
All tangled and distressed,
And her shoulders droop
under the morning's weight.

She rises and sighs,
Not noticing my eyes
Are completely, 100%
transfixed upon her:

Tired, struggling to rise,
With tired, fuzzy eyes,
Shuffling forth
to meet her coffee and her day.
And I smile,
Because she is mine.

Extra Sprinkles

The breakfast party of twelve
informs me another guest will be arriving–

At the head of the table,
a square-jawed, greyish-blond patriarch
(who reminds me of Adam West)
asks me to bring the new guest
a pink and white iced donut
with extra sprinkles.

I nod and smile politely,
then turn sharply on my heel,
passing through the swinging kitchen doors.

My eyes dart over the tray
of fresh-baked morning pastries,
placing the requested
pink and white iced donut
on a small china plate.

I hear a small rise in conversation
beyond the kitchen doors–
the arrival of the new guest.

Something prods the back of my mind,
like a guiding whisper.
Glancing to verify no one is watching,
I "borrow" heaping pinches of sprinkles
from all surrounding donuts:
star-shaped, round, oblong–
all in assorted rainbow colors.
I arrange them carefully,
letting them flow like dancing streams.

Re-entering the dining room,
I notice the new guest at once:
She is an eclectic beauty–
strawberry-blonde hair a bit disheveled,
wisps sneaking out from her braid
as if the wind had caught her unaware.

She wears a cornflower blue pullover,
an eggshell-colored shawl,
and brown Converse sneakers.
(I respect the choice of comfortable shoes.)

No makeup.
I sense she has nothing to hide,
but not in a self-absorbed kind of way–
she is just simply (effortlessly) herself.

She pushes back an errant curl
that falls before her black-rimmed glasses,
then smiles at the party,
draping the linen napkin on her lap.

My heart races–
I carefully, quietly,
place my gift in front of her.

She studies it a moment,
then exclaims:
"Extra sprinkles!"

I bow slightly
and reply, to my surprise,
"Only for you."

She blinks,
seeing me for the first time–
hazel-gray eyes locking with mine.
My heart skips a beat.

Then she offers
the simple, wonderful gift
of a broad, genuine,
(hopeful) smile.

Delay

My wife's focus ebbs and flows;
I notice the shift as she grows old.
Hints of silver highlight auburn hair–
she seldom notices my longing stare.

She speaks aloud, processing thoughts,
gathering and pruning them, like planted pots.
Some sprout or creep, others drift away–
some bloom into truths she seeks that day.

But I wait and listen: steady, unfazed–
content that her murmurs fill my days.
For I'd rather hear her, warm and near,
then bear the silence when she's not here.

Chinese Food Chatter (Our Third Date)

We begin with worn plates:
white patternless china,
noticeably heavy,
designed to be survivors
of scorching dishwasher cycles
and the test of time.

Soon, they overflow with noodles,
topped with crisp steamed vegetables,
a pyramid of sticky-sweet, deep-fried
General Tso's chicken,
and fluffy fried rice with scallions –
your favorite.

We instinctively test the savory aromas:
hints of ginger, fragrant sesame,
a touch of garlic and soy–
then smile, stirring in conversation,
light and playful banter
meant to linger.

"Why do we call them lazy susans," I ask,
spinning the duck sauce her way,
"when they're frequently moving?"
"Maybe", she replies, with a playful grin,
"It's because 'productive susans' just sounds silly."
I smile, thankful for her willingness to play.

Later, you twirl your ramen absentmindedly,
your glass waiting, empty, ice melting.
I sheepishly smile and blurt out:
"Maybe your Shirley Temple is late
because they're made from freshly squeezed Shirleys?"
You wipe a strand of hair from your cheek—
a small smile escapes.
My heart soars.

Dessert finds us quieter,
enjoying almond cookies and tea.
You excuse yourself for the restroom;
I fumble with "don't forget to send a postcard!"
You glance back, eyebrow arched in confusion –
I cringe at sabotaging myself.

After the awkwardness of the check, I wait,
hoping for an impossible sign.
"So…" you begin, pausing –
(I wait, my heart pounding.)
"….where do you want to go next week?"
And so, our banter turns to something new.

The Me in We

Thirteen minutes to midnight–
the train clatters past,
with the uniform clanking
of metal on metal:
clickety-clack, clickety-clack.

Overhead, dim lights blink
like tired, dull strobes,
rumbling in time
with the retreating train.

A dank mist creeps in
from the nighttime storm;
my coat clutches at me–
heavy, wet, and burdened.

I left the house hours ago,
with a roar and a crash.
We were stuck,
going nowhere good,
spinning in place.
A door slammed;
voices turned raw–

So, I left,
a ship unmoored,
bobbing through grief and rain,
until I drifted here–
fingers raw and stiff with cold,
chest uncomfortably warm,
watching the last train fade,
unsure where to go.

She declared me
"a willing victim of hostile lethargy"–
going through the motions,
purposely discontent,
unwilling to commit to anything
or any one –
"a casualty of self-inflicted transgressions."

And yet–
we had something.
Potential–
a fragile alchemy.
As a "we," we held more gravity
than I ever did alone.

On my own, I dismissed death
as just another function of time:
an inevitable, impersonal,
dehumanizing reality.
But in truth, it only frightened me
when I had something to lose.

Moisture glistens in thin webs
gathering around my boots,
reflecting the somber amber lights.
I hear distant speakers
droning on, sounding of tin,
performing "Let it Be"
as part of some arbitrary
24-hour loop.

I recall dancing in the kitchen,
her breath warm on my neck,
leek soup simmering,
biscuits warming in the oven,
Doctor Who queued up,
our lives briefly stitched together
in laughter and patchwork quilts.
A sublime, simple evening,
filled with smiles.
And us.

The truth is,
we all need to matter,
to be seen, needed, and loved.
We yearn for it.
It's not that complicated, really:
I need to find meaning in *"me"*
before I can uphold the weight of *"we"*.

I stare at the station's mouth,
rain tracing its shadowed edges.
Beyond it, the tracks vanish into the abyss–
five and a half hours until the next train.
I consider connecting with lost friends
dwelling nearby in Twickenham–
continuing my solace
in exchanges of brandy, burden,
and soft confessions.

But instead,
I measure my worth in silence,
then pull out my phone–
and decide to ask her
to come save me.

Clasped

Two pigeons,
Beaks clasped,
Heads bobbing:
Once –
Twice –
Parting,
Meeting again,
Repeating the ritual.

Steel gray heads,
Dark eyes shining–
Still, deep pools
Catching moonlight's glow.

Beaks touch,
Clasp again;
Heads sway and bob–
Briefly interlocked,
They are one.

I watch, transfixed:
Are they quarreling,
Or whispering secrets
Left untold?

Surely, this isn't the season
For tender affection—
Or, then again,
Maybe I am wrong,
As I take a moment
To recall your gaze this morning.

Homecoming

Seconds tick, a long and laborious click–
        one second….two….moments dragging
        like molasses, cold and thick.
Eyes burrow, my brow begins to furrow,
        trying to coax along the minutes
        as my mind calculates the miles home
        from Scarborough.
My stomach kicks, dancing with frenetic flips–
        feeling nervous, giddy, and warm,
        breathing quick and deep as my heart skips–
Today, my wife returns home from her trip.

Shifting from side to side, eyes darting outside,
        every 20 seconds, trying to bend time
        mentally decreasing the duration of the ride.
Waiting….four minutes….five….for my love to arrive.
        Over twenty years married,
        still eager like a child,
        waiting for her, anxiously,
        to return from her drive;
needing her to be with me, so I will once more be alive.

Too long, too late….a cruel twist of fate….
        wondering about the worst that could have
befallen,
        my mind spins and spirals and begins to debate
until her car pulls in, not a moment too late.

She steps to the door–
my truth is home–
and I begin to exist as *us* once more.

Be Mine (All Yours)

Valentine hearts
        (sappy stuff)
Hallmark hearts
        (full of fluff)
Hand-cut hearts
        (paper cuts)
Confectionery hearts
        (sugar rush)
Cupid's hearts
        (cherub's butt)
Chocolate hearts
        (spare-tire gut)
Flowing hearts
        (hopeless cause)
Open hearts
        (full of loss)
Broken hearts
        (empty without her transcendent smile....)

Humidity Hanging

Humidity hanging–
        pressing on my chest,
             heavy, stifling–
beneath the shroud of night.

The fan groans–
        tired of stirring stagnant air,
           musty, dank–
causing my chest to ache,
        fighting for labored breaths.

I peel away my blankets–
        soaked from sweat,
        smelling pungent and sharp–
           biting, like white vinegar.

Lying there,
        sprawled, exposed ,
           yearning for the slightest breeze–
           a whisper of relief.

The clock blinks
like ghoulish red eyes–
        10:24
        11:12
        11:53.
Dread creeps in:
        as morning inches closer, too soon.

I drag myself to the bathroom–
        a splash of cool water
        on my wrists and ankles,
           for a moment's reprieve.

Back in bed,
	my mind grasps for release–
		some small distraction,
		like a childhood lullaby,
	to ease me into slumber.

Then, I glance at her:
	beautiful, breathing easy,
	sleeping peacefully,
	untouched by the night.

And I find–
she is enough.

Things Unsaid

Dear John,
            the letter began quite innocently
I'm not sure how to really begin.
Lately, my heart has felt confused.
            no more so than my thoughts
            at your words
I know that I care deeply for you, but...
            ...but...
I think that I may have found another.
            and so my heart stops beating.
I never meant for it to happen.
            accidental murder, then?
He introduced himself as Rob.
            Rob...of course his name is Rob.
It was raining, and he offered me his umbrella.
            when it rains, it pours...
We walked...
            what did I do wrong?
and talked...
            what did I say that was wrong?
and soon, we became friends.
And eventually...
            ...please...no more...
we became something more.
I will always cherish our time together, John.
            she told me that our love was forever
And I hope that we can still be friends.
            I'd been saving for a ring.
Still, I hope--someday--you'll find it in your heart
to forgive me.
            With love,
            Jill

I stare at the lavender letterhead,
remembering a time when her notes
came folded with the scent
of lilacs in spring.

I sigh–
My hands tremble
as I put pen to paper.

Dear Jill,

**I received your note the other day. I want you
to know that I understand. All that I ever wanted
was for you to be happy. Love isn't something that
can be forced or faked; it must be pure and real. I
wish you the best, and all the luck for a bright future.
I know you will go far in life.**

Sincerely yours,

John

I slide the letter into an envelope,
my mind lost in what was
and in what will never be.
And then,
bowing my head into my hands,
I begin to cry–

Six Cents

The clock ticks, years ago–
in a tucked-away restaurant,
dimly lit, for an intimate moment.
The scene is set for this first date.

Six cents.
He reaches into the pocket
of his Sunday-pressed pants.
His fingers fumble,
brushing six thin coins.

His heart drops–
a heavy lump sinking into his stomach.
The truth sets in:
he cannot afford the meal.

The waiter lingers, eyebrow raised.
His foot taps impatiently–
judgment weighted
to the rhythm of a nearby clock.

The change is counted again–
clammy fingers twitch, dreading his undoing,
praying to repair
the ruined first impression.

A few dollars more–
or maybe a handful of change and some sympathy.
That's all it would take, to save this moment.
She rests her chin in her hands
hiding a bemused smile.
He cares–
awkwardly, yet sincerely.
That matters more than the meal.

Time drifts…
years wander on.
Wrinkles deepen,
well-worn from years of smiles–
a life builds quietly, happily,
as husband and wife.

More years pass–
she pours her second cup of morning coffee,
piping hot, with a bit of cream.
Her grandson is visiting
to settle his grandfather's affairs.

He sifts through memories:
photos, notes, odds and ends…
some feel like artifacts,
others more mundane.

Eventually, a question forms–
in a tin beside the bed,
he found two coins, simple and worn,
tucked in an old pillbox.

"A reminder," she laughs,
eyes deep yet still sparkling–
"a loan I gave your grandfather
many wonderful years ago,
to help him save his dignity."

Long ago, a life was built–
from a moment of grace,
six copper coins,
and the start of a promise.

Section 8. – Echoes

"Some people stay with you, long after they're gone."

Uneasy Teacher Slumber

She slumbers next to me, worn out,
recovering from the day–

She said goodbye to a student today,
someone she poured her soul into,
now tossed to an uncertain home,
miles away from all he's known.

She mourns for them–
each one.

Too often, they're cast about–
subjected to the whims
of insecure adults–
treated like accessories,
seen as burdens,
counted as data points
to serve some agenda–
when what they really need
is to be held.

She prays for them,
individually,
every day,
until she loses count,
and has to start over.

Tonight, she turns in her sleep and sighs–
So, I pray instead for her,
hoping tomorrow
she can find strength
to love those who remain.

Metal

She pauses at the door to her grandfather's body shop,
digging for hidden reserves of strength,
though her knees betray her.

She hates this place—
the stench of motor oil fused with cheap bourbon,
a mix that could explode under a cutting torch
or under his temper,
which flares just as wild and hot.

Somewhere inside, metal whines and groans,
crying like a song no one remembers how to play.
This is where he spends his days–
bent over broken things,
surrounded by screaming metal,
alone in a solitary
no one dares disturb.

He doesn't care for endings.
He likes to start things—

Sometimes, he starts projects:
resurrecting metal, rebuilding mangled cars,
cutting his hands against the work
as if he needs the pain.

Other times, he starts arguments–
bullying a disagreement into submission
with his brutish size and bluster.

She wonders what madness
brought her here alone.

She steps inside.
The hairs on her neck bristle–
an unseen voltage climbing her spine.

In the back, past curtains of rusted chains
and hooks twisted like broken smiles,
she sees him–
torch in hand, goggles down,
his bald head catching the light,
sparks flickering across his beard
like dying stars.

She waits—
barely breathing,
waiting to be acknowledged.

The torch carves a crooked arc through a fender.
She exhales
almost painfully,
watching his violent ballet.

Finally, he stops.
Goggles lift.
She receives a disapproving, questioning glance.

She lifts the lunch pail he left at home,
trying not to tremble,
daring not to speak.

He nods toward a nearby workbench,
grunts,
and turns back to the flame.

No words.
No "thanks." No "hello."
Just a nod and a growl,
then the hiss of the torch reigniting.

She nods in return,
turns,
and walks fast without running–
not daring to seem afraid.

As she leaves his personal corner of hell,
she tries to remember
what he was like
before her grandmother passed.

Was there kindness in his eyes?
Or tenderness in his huge hands?

For a moment, the fear softens,
giving way to something else–
a heavy pity
for the angry man
she no longer knows.

My Friend Charlie

My friend Charlie died today;
it was a mix of bipolar and addiction, they say,
that ultimately led him astray–
my friend Charlie took his life today.

My friend Charlie was often down;
he was always looking to be found,
instead of being referred to as "what a clown"–
my friend Charlie is no longer around.

Life gave Charlie only rocks;
we slowly preyed on him with all our mocks.
He eventually caved to all our squawks–
our talk condemned him to a box.

My friend Charlie died today;
it was his own fault, is what they say.
Me, I see it another way….

Myths, Eclipse

Our ancestors believed in magic—
they crafted myths
to name the unknown
and conjured legends
to guard against fear.

For thousands of years,
it was a comforting,
terrifying system of creativity,
bound by wonder and ignorance—
explaining the phenomena
of everyday extraordinary life:
Raijin's thunder,
Persephone's seasons,
and a thousand more tales of the world.

Myth unveiled the inexplicable nature of eclipses.
Some described demons, monsters, or beasts
seeking to devour the sun—
for conquest,
immortality,
or celestial battles
of terrifying grandeur.

Others whispered of passionate lovers—
blanketing the sun and moon in their embrace,
causing the world to tremble
in the thrill of their union.

They were tales of insatiable hunger,
of cosmic balance and symbolic struggle,
of mischievous gods,
and unknowable mystery.

They were stories of *us*.

Somewhere along the line,
science took over.
Still,
I allow nature's beauty to take shape:

Sitting on my porch,
breathing the earthy weight
and whispering ozone of a storm–

Taking in the quiet interlude
of a snowy day
or the tender embrace
of summer warmth–

Marveling at the cosmic ballet
of light and darkness–
an eclipse painting the world,
as seen through protective glasses
that are a distant relative
of Steve Ruskin's Eclipse-o-scope.

Father Mahoney

Barbels bang–
metal clashing against metal,
echoing off squat racks,
all drenched in sweat and 80's death rock.

Father Mahoney tries to break his record,
knowing he will need a long shower
before the 4pm Mass.
Five more reps–
that's what he is praying for.

He read last night about the Four Chaplains,
selfless men of different faiths
who gave their lives in 1943
as the USS Dorchester sank.
They guided desperate sailors
until lifejackets ran out–
then gave away their own.

As the ship slipped beneath the waves,
sailors heard the mix of prayers–
English, Latin, and Hebrew–
still urging them to safety.

Mahoney pauses to spot one young man–
twenty, maybe,
arms sleeved in gang ink
dragging his regrets through each rep,
eyes locked on the bar
like it is the only thing pulling him forward.

Today, he's one of many–
men searching for some purpose,
needing the connection of this gym.

Father Mahoney wasn't always a weightlifter–
today he seeks to beat his personal record,
not for himself,
but to entice these men to come to mass.

So, he picks up the bar again,
arms shaking, shoulders screaming–
if four strangers
from different backgrounds and faiths
could die for sailors they barely knew,
then he can survive a bit of pain
if it might bring these young men
something more than just a sermon.

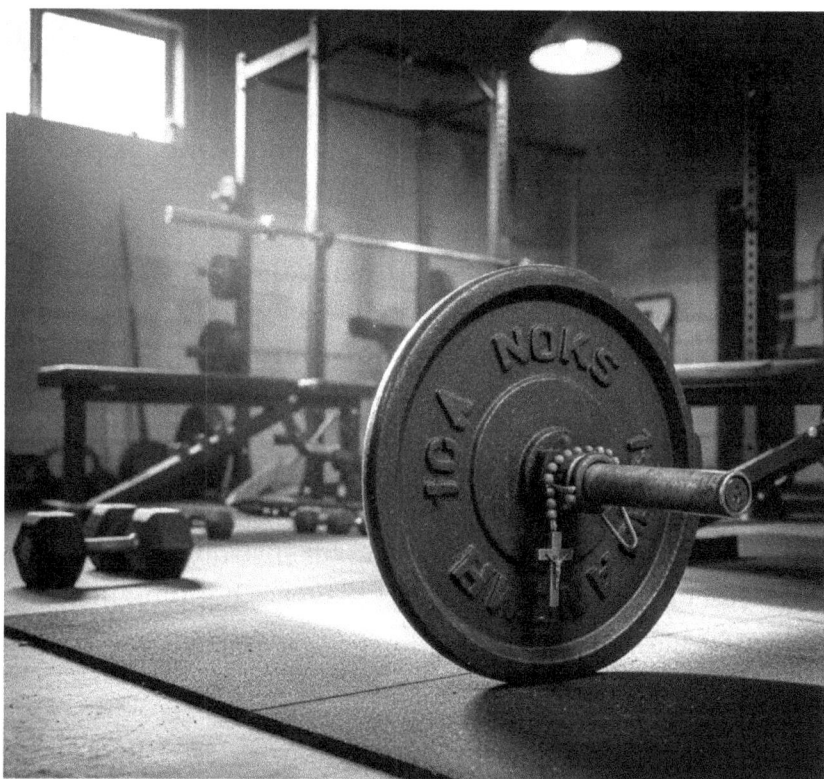

Bobby Plays

Bobby McFerrin shuffles onto the stage–
dressed in slender black jeans and a matching t-shirt,
his grey-haired dreads float across his shoulders
as he lifts a thin arm to acknowledge the crowd
with a wave, then a peace sign.

Bobby sits, taking a sip from a white china tea cup,
the crowd still roaring, a coronation heralding his arrival,
as the band forms around him: bass (upright), percussion,
guitar, trumpet, supporting vocals–
all smooth yet lively, like the music they are about to play.
From Charlestown, the jazz-infused group Ranky Tanky,
topping charts, shining stars,
pleased to play a supporting role to Bobby.

Bobby stands and warms up his throat–
it starts as a series of high sing-songy bops and beeps
before dropping into the lower register,
then dancing somewhere in the middle.
Soon, his warm-up evolves, growing into the melody,
a wordless vocal opera, all produced by Bobby;
the band smiles and soon starts to play along.

Bobby sings, smiling–
for a moment, I swear I hear a trumpet
and have to check (twice) to confirm
that the trumpet player is resting his instrument on his knee;
instead of playing, the trumpet player is bopping his head,
waving his hand,
and singing along with Bobby.
Soon, Bobby waves his own hands,
gesturing us to join in the chorus,
and all of us in the theater become part of the same band.

Bobby pauses, then speaks–
he asks the band "what does Ranky Tanky actually mean?"

They smile and reply it comes from a Gullah expression
roughly translated as "get funky",
the spiritual guiding soul of the group.
They begin to play, illustrating Ranky Tanky's meaning–
Bobby stares, for long moments,
as the guitar player's fingers dance across strings;
Bobby then laughs, and joins in,
his voice is another instrument
in a powerful orchestra of funk and passion.

Bobby continues into the night;
I listen, transfixed, wondering which parts are rehearsed,
practiced perfection,
and which portions are improvised,
living extensions from his soul.
It is as if when God created us
he plucked a single piece of His hair,
looked at Bobby,
and said: "Use this for your voice".

Bobby stops–
and the crowd roars once again.
He thanks us, then pauses to answer questions
and share a few more lasting moments of his time.
When asked if he still practices, Bobby replies
"A little bit here, a little bit there...but it all adds up",
then laughs along with us.
Bobby thanks us once again, and asks for healing thoughts–
he shares he has Parkinson's but believes in prayer,
what he calls "Vitamin P", the most powerful cure,
and suddenly I want to cry.
He bows and waves once more–
we cheer,
and then Bobby shuffles off the stage.

For Lois
("Superman's Sonnet")

I never knew my birth home. Sent away
when I was just a child — "for love," they claim.
I found a farm, a city, and a name,
but still the hurt, though faded, stays today.

I'm part of them, but who I am was grown
on that farm, where I was raised on what's true:
to honor all that's sacred and atone.
Still, one thing was absent and missing– you.

I watch, over wire-rimmed frames with care:
raven-haired, fierce, and kind, your spirit rare.
You work, unknowing of the gifts you share:
you make me stronger–lift me through the air.
Son, visitor, protector, man – unsure –
finally home, as long as I am *yours*.

Section 9. – The Inner Life

"I feel the same: stuck somewhere between seasons."

A Loss of Two

She lost the twins today.
This was not the fairy tale ending life had intended,
especially not after what was considered
a routine check-up.
She had gone in feeling an odd pain–
at first hot and acidic,
like a night eating too many spicy enchiladas,
followed by an indescribable churning twist.

Now, she sits alone,
surrounded by the distinct, sterile smell
of hospital antiseptic,
too adrift in unreality to care about the immodesty
of her half-open gown.
Monitor cables taped to her chest–
pulsating, ironic electronic beats
echoing the whispers of physicians in the hall.

All that remains in her is emptiness–
an unnatural calm, matched by a vacant uterus.
She thinks to herself with drifting, misplaced regret,
desperately grasping
for something tangible to latch onto,
that someone will need to take down
the double swings hanging in the backyard,
and what an inconvenience that will be,
especially with the recent drab weather.

Move On

I am weary–
sometimes I yearn to let go,
give up this weight, this world,
unravel, drift into silence,
and move on.

But I know if I do,
part of them goes too–
lost in misplaced blame
for choices not their own.

They would be made less–
victims of my fragile disposition,
my longing to disappear.
So I hold on,
daring to endure.

Dismissed

From the intercom, announcements blare–
electronic static grates my ears
like gravel grinding against rusty gears,
nerves shatter like exploding glassware.

Students scatter like crazed barnyard chickens.
Information drowning in seas of voices,
unheard, unnoticed, all facts lost choices,
as no student-chicken ever listens.

Notes left scattered, paperwork forgotten–
at home, the plea is "not my fault!"
as if permission slips were locked in some vault
or were plans most vile and rotten.

Hapless teachers linger dazed, subdued...
in their private, self-inflicted servitude.
Soon students return to start anew,
hands outstretched, grasping paperwork like glue.

Contentment

Madness is living in absolutes,
Wallowing between perfection and desperation,
Grasping at extremes that don't exist.

Some people thrive on turning others sour,
A petty vendetta on flaws they think they see.
Madness is living in absolutes.

Others build their empires on those they've devoured,
Chasing the best car, wife, or family for grace,
Grasping at extremes that don't exist.

"Perfection" is an illusion—crafted and contrived,
A figment of "happily ever after" and flawless skin.
Madness is living in absolutes.

Some seek the unattainable, searching desperately for
The picture-perfect home, faultless job, or textbook life,
Grasping at extremes that don't exist.

In truth, there can be serenity in "almost perfect".
There is contentment in striving for your personal best.
Madness is living in absolutes,
Grasping at extremes that don't exist.

As Luck Would Have It

The key to good luck is a unique recipe–
It takes one part opportunity and one part effort.
It needs a pinch of randomness
Along with heaping spoonfuls of
Sweat, pain, and sleepless nights.

To that, gently fold in generous amounts
Of being at the right place at the right time.
Sprinkle in both privilege and happenstance,
And then toss in handfuls of hard work.
(I promise it won't spoil the batter.)

Measure out even, gentle cups of gratitude,
With dashes of mindfulness and happiness.
Add in a teaspoon of calculated risk,
Then blend well into a large open mind.
Let the mixture simmer and sit.

The tastiest versions of luck are always
Part circumstance and part devotion,
Although I'm also fond of an occasional bite
Of pure blind dumb luck.

My Beautiful Lutein

Sitting in the optometrist's office,
with my appointment not quite upon us,
my eyes spy a sign about lutein–
which, I learn, helps with all that is seen.

Lutein, I learn, can be found
where leafy green veggies abound,
and, with zeaxanthin, can make
"internal sunglasses" for eyesight's sake,
protecting them from oxidative stress
and blocking harsh light's damaging caress.

The poster praises vitamins A and E,
with free radical protection for you and me.
Copper and zinc are listed as well,
but again–lutein still sounds mighty swell.

Nevertheless, I must confess,
you spoke with disarming distress
when I lauded "Lutein" as a name–
and suggested our baby be called the same.

Quite pregnant, you provided a labored sigh–
"I see you and I don't see eye to eye,
and while I hate to defy, my final reply?
No, I don't think so. Nice try."

And so, into the eye exam, I go.
My beautiful Lutein gone–although,
maybe...just maybe...I can convince my queen
to name our daughter a lovely "Irene".

Black Hole Solution

My uncle, the astrophysicist, came to visit–
a stoic gentleman with a thick peppered beard,
he smelled of pipe tobacco and tweed.

For his vacation, he endeavored three things,
as noted on the "to do list" he posted on our
refrigerator:
- Catch up on columns of "light" reading,
- Wax nostalgic with my "little brother",
- Sincerely flatter my sister-in-law's home
  cooking.

I came home Thursday filled with anxious butterflies,
unsure if I had made a catastrophic mistake
auditioning for the school's annual play.

I felt ordinary, insignificant, full of doubt–
what right did I have trying to be a star?
My uncle listened, stroking his heavy beard,
glancing at me absently over his book.

"Everyone wants to be a star," he murmured,
his voice like gravel mixed with molasses,
"when they should wish to be a black hole."

I reflexively roll my eyes–
he countered by clearing his throat.
"It is simple science," he stated,
a thin, satisfied smile lurking beneath his beard.

"Stars shine;
they become sonnets and songs.
But blackholes remain wonderfully unique–
beautifully misunderstood."

He continued, closing his book,
yet still holding the feel of academia around him:
"Blackholes are invisible regions of space
with gravity so strong that nothing,
not even the brightest star's light,
can escape them.
They draw entire worlds."

He leaned forward, locking my eyes–
his glance softened,
an odd mix of knowledge and personal regret.

"Black holes are mysterious and fascinating–
they remind us that beauty
is not always understood.
They prove even the unseen
can have huge impacts."

I smile, nodding,
holding his words close,
a gift from a man
I feel I barely know.

"Don't allow others to define your existence–"
he leaned back,
retreating to the mysteries of his book–
a well-worn hardback by Katie Mack,
"The End of Everything (Astrophysically Speaking")).

Glancing one last time over his book,
he hid a smile, then continued:
"But also avoid collapsing the rest of the world
into your event horizon..."

192

The scale mocks me with a reality of my own making–
192.

Digital numbers,
cold and unyielding,
red block digits,
square-edged and graceless,
lacking the courtesy of a curve–
192.

The toll of being home-bound:
a home office, home cooking,
living and working within the same four walls,
days folding into evenings,
all blurring into weeks–
tension rising,
good habits eroding,
bad ones rumbling like rapid tides–
192.

I sigh–
Then grab my coat to go for a walk,
hoping tomorrow to find the strength
to endure the monotony
without chasing the fleeting joy
of a nibble of carbs,
a morsel of sweets,
just to return to–
184.

An Off Day

I awoke, feeling obligated to write–
honing one's craft requires time,
and poetry, when deeply nourished,
needs persistence and labor to shine.

I did not want to write of death;
that well's been drawn too deep.
Nor ponder endings or new beginnings;
I'd let that chapter rest this week.

I considered love, as I am a big fan;
Feeling inadequate, I found little to say.
I considered writing about nature's beauty,
but then decided to wait another day.

I wondered, then, what was left to tell?
An ode to an Adirondack chair?
A limerick about an old fishing hat?
A sonnet about a picnic basket and bear?
A haiku on a dung beetle, lonely and fat?

With that, I decided to take the day off–
to recharge myself, my pen at rest,
and admit I had nothing to say.
Sometimes, the poet must pause the quest
to simply live their life for a day.

Section 10. – Even Flow

"The air feels like a promise to live another day."

William Carlos Williams

Waiting between patients
in his Rutherford office,
the doctor taps his pencil,
thinking–

Next to him sits
an appreciated
but half-eaten
chicken-salad sandwich,
which should be the occupation of this,
his lunch,
instead of poetry.

With the slight promise of a smile,
the doctor grabs a prescription pad,
and,
with quick, loose strokes,
writes about
a red wheelbarrow.

Dickinson

Upon entering the library
on an unassuming Monday evening,
near dusk in autumn–

I meander dimly lit,
sometimes-forgotten rows,
seeking truth
amongst the many-tome stacks.

Dickinson comes to me
in the form of a haiku:

On library shelves
Emily Dickinson sits–
breaking rules. (Maybe).

Sunday, Maine

Overcast skies, vacationing in Maine,
lazy showers casting doubts on the day,
I attend Sunday service
in an unfamiliar church.

I shift awkwardly in the mass, alone,
aware of wayward glances from locals
for sitting in their pew, seven rows back.

Through an open stained-glass window,
the rain, cool and even, smells of the sea,
even though we are miles away from the coast.

Soon I hear about Job in the whirlwind,
with the ocean bursting forth from a womb,
and I know I too can weather the storm.

Upon a poem

It is infinitely more difficult
to write
with a cat
on your lap.

But–
it can have
its equal rewards.

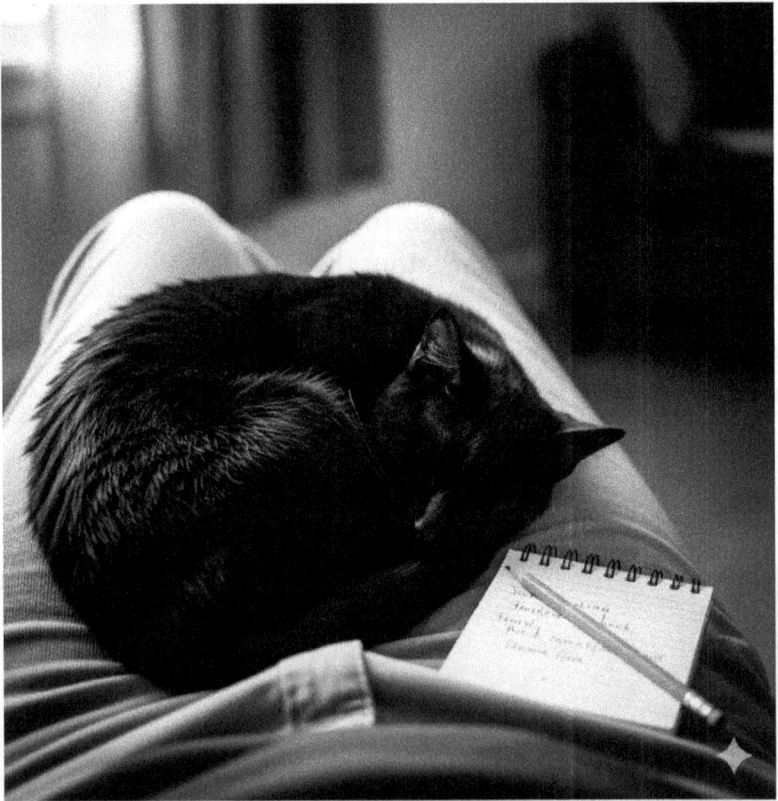

Scholar Brawler James Morrow

Scholar brawler James Morrow
poet pugilist, doctor of letters
followed his father into the ring
despite protests he remain at university–
to focus on books instead of right hooks.

Within a month, men spoke of Dr. Morrow:
light on his feet, with a mean left jab,
well-spoken and well-read,
sipping either warm tea or neat gin,
always respectfully sweet to the midnight ladies.

By three months, Dr. Morrow went on tour,
visiting libraries in every city where he fought,
ruining local champions with decisive wins,
always apologizing to their mothers after the match.

By year's end, on an unassuming day,
he won the world title with little personal fanfare–
hardly considering the shifts at play.

Life became a whirlwind of bouts and cities in brief –
no time for museums, or well-traveled reads.
By year two, the twinkle left his eyes,
a scholar's fire dimmed under fame's weight.

The end came as a relief.
In the first round, he was lithe and quick,
dodging sharp jabs, putting in licks.
By the second round, his knees began to sway;
he longed for his books, for simpler days,
for deeply-pooled thoughts by the old elm tree.

When he went down in the third, lights going dim,
Plato's words echoed, thick like blood:
"the measure of a man is what he does with power…"

High School Love and Edgar Allen Poe

"Once upon a midnight dreary,"
    once said Poe, so very clearly,
    as I dozed in English class
    dreaming of one that I hold dearly.

"Over many a quaint and curious volume of forgotten lore-"
    my eyes wandered toward the open door
    searching for some idle distraction,
    trying to subdue an errant snore.

"From my books surcease of sorrow - sorrow for the lost Lenore-"
    In the hallway, the one I secretly adore
    wandered by with stunning beauty,
    "Nameless here forevermore."

"Presently my soul grew stronger;"
    my eyelids drooped in sleep no longer
    as the one I had adored from afar
    drew ever closer, my heart along her.

"Deep into that darkness peering,"
    to the door my love was nearing–
    I wondered what words could win her,
    while stupid utterances were what I was fearing.

"But the silence was unbroken,"
    as my heart remained unspoken–
    my beloved took her seat not knowing
    of my unending, affectionate token.

"Back into the chamber turning,"
    my true love had left me yearning,
    for a chance to express what I feel,
    the great passion within me burning.

"In there stepped a stately Raven of saintly days of yore,"
      Poe's verse continued to be a bore,
      distracting me from the beauty three aisles over,
      causing me to want her even more.

"Ghastly grim and ancient Raven wandering"
      my mind continued upon its pondering,
      hoping that the "Nevermore"
      wouldn't start my heart to floundering.

"Much I marveled this ungainly fowl to hear discourse so plainly"
      my desire for her was growing insanely
      when my love turned slightly toward me
      and passed a smile in no way blandly.

"Till I scarcely more than muttered"
      with her smile, my heart truly fluttered;
      I tried to reply with a confident "hi",
      although I think I may have stuttered.

"Caught from some unhappy master,"
      my teacher caught my attention faster
      by telling me to quit my daydreaming,
      turning my hopes into disaster.

"Then, upon the velvet sinking,"
      my embarrassment got me to thinking,
      my teacher's presence could cause further problems:
      the situation was definitely stinking.

"This I sat engaged in guessing"
      how best to go about expressing
      my undying love for this smiling girl
      apart from Poe's insistent pressing.

"Then, methought, the air grew denser"
　　　as my nerves grew ever tenser,
　　　realizing the period was approaching end,
　　　the truth stabbing me like a vicious fencer.

"On this home by Horror haunted-"
　　　my hopes drew up to be undaunted
　　　I would declare my love for this girl today;
　　　my feelings would finally be completely flaunted!

"By that God we both adore,"
　　　I knew there was nothing I wanted more,
　　　so, I gathered my possessions and my wits
　　　as the bell let out a mighty roar.

"Quote the Raven, 'Nevermore'"
　　　the words rambled as I stopped her by the door,
　　　but when I went to express my love,
　　　all I could utter was one name, "Lenore…"

"And the Raven, never flitting,"
　　　proved to be my reason for quitting
　　　trying to express my feelings of love,
　　　and has left me to be still sitting, still sitting.

The First Sunday of Lent

It is snowing in March on the first Sunday in Lent,
    about one week shy of the spring equinox.
Not a gentle, peaceful snow
    with plump floating flakes fluttering lazily
    like a pantomime of playful, silent tumblers,
but instead a fierce, biting snow,
    with stinging white daggers jabbing vertically,
    whipping the air into a chaotic circus
    of frenzied motion.

Sitting in church,
    staring out the window at the snow,
    losing focus of the pastor
    to the violent ballet beyond,
I decide what I want to sacrifice this spring for Lent
    is winter.

April's Rainstorm

Daybreak–
before the sticky sweat and heat
settle over Alabama.
April rises, patting her eyes
with heirloom embroidered cotton–
red already from the sleepless night.

"April's Rain Song,"
her momma used to call it
whenever April cried–
not with malice,
but to coax a smile.

April packs her black dress–
she knows her sister
will be dressed in red.

"When Sue wears red,"
Momma would say,
"It's like a sunset sliding into the room."
April never understood
how the end of something
could be beautiful–
but Momma did.

Sue would be cursing the day already;
"Bad morning," she would mutter.
"Bad morning…"
April, a quiet girl,
readies herself instead
for what must come:
acceptance.

That is what Momma would want;
not weary blues
dragging through the hours
like your emotions were a heavy wet coat.
She would not want denial
robbing us of healing.

Momma would want acceptance:
that rare moment when life feels right–
as we focus on what we had,
and how much better it made us,
instead of what we have lost.

April closes her eyes,
counting the hours the bus will take
to carry her from Alabama back home
for a night funeral in Harlem–
a chance to say goodbye to Momma,
and that first step
back toward living.

Tides

Cascading sands, fanned browns and tans–
gritty yet smooth, like invisible sheets of summer dew.
Beaches stretch–rolling stretches of silent lands,
reaching for tides to shape timeless sands–
the shore kissing seas of shimmering greys and blues.

The air carries the slight taste of sea-born brine.
Tidal marshes, with green fingers grasping living pools,
surrounded by powdered-sugar sand, bright and fine.
Waves, like skittering cat paws, dance and climb–
nature erasing all evidence of hubris and rules.

Houses dot the coast: bright whites, pale blues, mixed
grays–
rising against the moving tapestry of the sea.
They sit like man-made rocks across the bay,
built to endure all seasons–night and day–
steadfast and unmoved, unlike the persistent sea.

Oceans drift like forgotten memories–
Beaches sigh; landscapes rearrange.
Static homes solemnly watch living seas.
Life rolls on, as oceans shape all I see–
leaving me to wait for the tides to change.

Section 11. – The Long Road Home

"Sometimes the bravest thing to do is simply to live."

Loose Ball

It glances, skimming past my fingertips.
My knee twists–hard. It pops, then slides back in place.
My teeth grit. I rise, full of stubborn pride.
I race, knee screaming for relief. A shot–
Two points. I play, then pause to ice. No pain….

Years roll on. College ends: graduation.
Marriage, then kids–other games begin.
They grow and play; I sit now in the stands.
I cringe at every dive for a loose ball–
yet cheer, as those old days still call to me.

Thirty years later, I stretch twice a day.
On humid nights, it swells and lightly throbs.
It robs me, leaving sleepless, aching nights.
I still play sometimes in my dreams–for pride.
The memory endures each day, with pain.
But still, I smile–from love.

Martha's Diner

The morning crowd gathers at Martha's Diner,
bellying up to the counter, perched on chrome stools.
Here, beneath the glow of a neon "open" sign,
I discover the totality of life and all its hidden rules.

A gentleman in Sunday best and light peppered hair,
concentrates intently on his granddaughter's soccer story.
His face, deep and worn, shows all his life's trials,
yet he sits, sipping coffee, unbitter, living in her glory.

A young woman in an oversized *Visit Anchorage* sweatshirt
swirls at her eggs, eyes locked intently on her companion's
face.
Soon, laughter erupts–as she watches with knowing eyes,
as her toast is stolen with playful grace.

They come for omelets, bacon, and momentary connection:

a woman browsing bridal magazines for the perfect dress;
her fiancé, glancing at game highlights to relieve his stress;
old friends who argue over local politics as life's greatest
gift;
the nurse, yawning over a bagel after her overnight shift;
the man, circling "help wanted" ads, afraid to tell his wife–
Then there is me, seeking my last meal before ending my
life….

I came to forget, to enjoy my final breakfast,
to disappear in pancakes before slipping away.
But witnessing this world—this simple, unfolding life—
I hesitate, lingering in the moment, and decide to stay.

Somewhere In-Between

It creeps up on me,
one gray, unassuming Saturday
during my weekend ritual:
mechanically dragging
our groaning Electrolux behind me.

Then it hits–
an unexpected wave of depression,
a twisting knot, low in my gut,
followed by an acidic burn in my chest.

My fingertips twitch,
pulsating with electric twinges,
as I fight for a steady breath.

Behind the wall,
the washer hums
causing cabinet glasses
to tinkle like wind chimes.
The furnace soon joins in,
with a low, rumbling growl.

My thoughts scatter,
ping-ponging through triggers:

Is it the dripping faucet
that I don't know how to fix?
Or the dumb argument earlier
over the empty cat litter bag?

Maybe it was the clash with my daughter?
Me threatening to banish her phone,
her glaring at me in scorn,
her eyes full of fire and silence–
I miss her carefree laughs.

146

Or maybe it was breakfast,
as my son quietly confessed,
at seventeen,
he sometimes lies awake
worrying about death.
I sat there,
wondering how the world
had dimmed his dreams.

Maybe it was all of that
or something else….
or nothing at all.

Outside, the yard hangs in limbo,
caught between late autumn
and early frost–
cold, bare, and waiting.
I feel the same:
stuck somewhere between seasons.

For a moment,
I consider giving in–
but my stubbornness wins out.

I swallow hard.
With a flick of the button,
the Electrolux returns–
its steady humming becomes
a small reminder
to carry on.

Bird's Eye View

I spied a little bird one day,
it seemed to look at me—
perched so still, surveying the world
from the bough of a sycamore tree.

I gave it a wink and a curious smile,
watching it bob its head;
I wondered what secrets it might reveal,
what mysteries might be said?

"Hello, little bird!" I called with cheer,
"tell me, what do you see?
Is the world a wonder, vast and bright,
from your throne in the sycamore tree?

Do you unravel the universe's threads?
Do you ponder the near and far?
Do you understand life's secret riddles,
and all that's wondrously bizarre?"

The bird just blinked, as if to reply,
"your questions are quite profound."
Then it took off with a fluttering leap,
traversing without a sound.

But just as I smiled and tipped my hat,
its answer arrived from the sky–
a pinpoint reply, both swift and precise:
white droppings landed in my eye.

I gasped and winced, shaking my fist,
then groaned, wiping the mess away.
but soon I sighed, for life, I thought,
is often messy that way.

"Some days are miracles," I then resolved,
"while others leave their mark, I see.
So, I'll learn and will grow, weathering all storms—
but possibly avoid the sycamore tree."

The Birth of the Milky Way
(as Seen on a Tuesday Morning)

She begins with a flick of her wrist,
sending a wave of almost unseen,
seemingly ancient chalk dust cascading before her,
drifting softly from her hand like a personal Milky Way.
My teacher's eyes dart and flash, kinetic and bright,
as she unravels the mysteries of the galaxy.

She bounds through gravitationally bound systems
with the frantic energy of a gazelle,
rushing past stellar remnants, exotic quarks, compact stars–
brilliant flashes of energy, absence, and color.
She advances past bits of dancing dust,
spiraling toward black holes,
then smirks knowingly at some interstellar gas.

Next, she glances at hypothetical, invisible dark matter,
and–unflinching–
stares down the majestic purple and orange explosions
of a supernova giant
collapsing into a neutron star.
The image is breathtaking and unspeakable–
a wonder eyes appreciate,
but my mind cannot truly comprehend.

Next to me, my classmate yawns,
straining to keep his eyes open
in our second-period astronomy class
on this uncommonly warm Tuesday in October.

Therein lies proof–
passion is magnificent and powerful,
yet not always contagious.

Life (in the Tank)

The fish pump grinds with a mechanical hum–
rhythmic, low grumbles
interspersed between fleeting,
almost indistinguishable pauses–
quick, deep snarls
forever circulating the tank's surface
into cascading bubbles.

Watching the mesmerizing,
churning ballet of water,
I wonder if the fish loathe
the rasping whine of the pump
or mourn the deafening solitude
when, occasionally, it goes silent?

The Long Way Here

This week, both our kids
left home for college.

Our daughter, a freshman,
journeyed to school
with butterflies the size of pterodactyls
flapping wildly about her stomach.

Campus was a frenzy–
first-year students,
flush with nervous eagerness–
a parade of boxes and minifridges
marching to awaiting dorms.

We lingered,
upon unspoken insistence,
to find a special place for every item:
a specific desk drawer for pencils;
a perfect windowsill for succulents;
a spot to charge her phone.

Then, she crept out–
timid steps forward,
smiling politely when someone–
equally unsure–
asked about lunch.

My wife, to her credit,
held it together
until we made it to the car.
Then she sobbed–
not for our daughter,
but at her own change in purpose.
She was still her mother,
but something unspoken shifted.

Two days later, our son–
a senior–
left home with the ease
of familiar routine.

His car was packed to the roof:
faded blue bins of kitchenware;
duct-taped boxes bursting at the seams;
an old lamp peering from one window
like an eager child.

After eighteen years of school,
stretching back to paper stars
and preschool blocks,
he was approaching the final stretch.

A knot formed in my chest,
tight beneath my heart,
as his car left the driveway–
I'd always be his father,
but this might have been
his last summer home.

And then, there were two.
Just us again–
young lovers,
sporting a touch of grey,
still wondering and looking
where life might lead us.

The Last Song

As my last note fades,
echoing–
I hear applause,
like distant, warm-summer thunder,
surrounding me,
as I stand among the gathered stars.

I see Him– smiling,
light dancing on His face,
aglow in the vast abyss
of the great unknown crowd.

My breath catches,
leaving me momentarily,
gathering in the moment…
an ovation!

I bow, deeply,
meeting His eyes once more–
then, enveloped with contentment,
like a lingering, comforting hug,
I exit the stage
to return home.

The Ballad of Kevin Von Erich

They say the Pacific holds no memory–
he considers this, here in paradise,
on one of the great Hawaiian Islands,
where tides wash away the past.

His name is Kevin Ross Adkisson,
but the world knows him as Kevin Von Erich,
the barefoot boy in a family of gods,
Texas royalty in spandex and sweat,
cheered by thousands under golden lights.

His family was the Kennedys of Texas:
smiling, handsome, all-American–
rock-star celebrities, cheered and beloved,
a professional wrestling dynasty
from the heart of the American Southwest.

Once he was the second of six brothers–
now he is the last who remains.
Jack, the oldest, drowned at age six;
David passed far from home
while performing in Japan;
Kerry, Mike, and Chris lost their silent battles,
all victims of pressure and fame.

When David died overseas in 1984,
the state mourned:
schools closed, the legislature recessed,
thousands lined the streets
in solemn, stunned procession.

When Kerry passed in 1993,
he did so alone:
by a .44 caliber bullet
on his father's ranch
in the hush of a golden field –
no crowd, no cameras,
just open Texas sky.

Fame has a way of making one less:
the individual consumed
by the vision of the crowd.
Some never recover,
while others are left to heal.

On Sunday, now in his 60's,
Kevin climbs barefoot up his favorite tree,
carrying a well-worn machete,
to gather and enjoy a fresh papaya.
He calls this his "office"–
it's where he goes to think.

On Monday, he goes scuba diving
and lies at the bottom of the ocean,
surrounded by quiet, living peace.

On Tuesday, he pauses by an old photo:
an image of him and his brothers–
a match with the Fabulous Freebirds
in Fort Worth, Texas on July 4th, 1984.
He recalls how hot it was that day,
and how smoky-yet-sweet
the barbecue was after the show.

On Wednesday, he rises to a peach sunrise
on the early morning,
and dines on Kona crab in the evening.

On Thursday, he herds sheep
in the sublime green pastures
of the lower meadow.

Friday, surrounded by his grandchildren,
they wade and play
on the waters of the Kalihiwai River.
Their laughter eases his soul.

On Saturday, he watches his sons
wrestling in the jungle:
strong like his older brother,
handsome like his little brother,
quick like he was in his younger days,
smiling like he and his brothers once did,
and he wonders–

They claim what took his brothers
was "the Von Erich Curse".
He thinks about that, here in paradise,
living off the land,
with three generations near,
and considers:

sometimes the bravest thing to do
is simply to live.

Appendix:
To All Things...

Alas, an Introduction

This poem is about me,
which is why I don't trust it.
Introductions are necessary, I suppose,
but I approach them like a three-day-old salad—
wilting, overdressed,
forgotten in the back of the fridge,
until desperation calls.

With that warning in place:

I am a fourth-generation Vermonter,
rooted in the Northeast Kingdom,
where seasonal beauty and brutal honesty
walk hand in hand.
I admire our quirky artisans,
sincere farmstands,
and fence-post tales.
I mirror this place's stubborn resolve,
caught between progress and nostalgia.

I married a city girl
far out of my league,
and fathered two kids
whom I (somehow) didn't ruin.
When I'm not working,
I am mowing, raking, or shoveling—
depending on the season.

There should be more to say–
but the locals value silence.
As such, when pondering myself,
it feels that less is more.

Acknowledgements and Idle Thoughts

I seek more than a meager life—
not in possessions, gathering dust,
but in the curating of people and days,
shaping who I become.

I offer these thanks,
and a few stray reflections,
for what has carried my writing.

To this small town
where I live, labor, dream, fail:
thank you for whispering me home
when I wander too far,
and for making me wonder
if there is more.

To the strangers I will never meet:
if I misinterpret you, forgive me–
I seek to honor, not infringe,
the unique unknown of who you are.

To my wife:
thank you for adventures
and sorry for the mess.
(You knew what you were getting into.)

To my kids:
seek your own voices—
they will shine brighter than mine.
Also, clean your rooms.
(Yes, even as adults.)

To my family yet-to-be:
thank you for listening patiently
to the struggling old man
who loses the days
yet still remembers
enough stories to tell.

Like Whitman, I contain multitudes—
fragments of people and places.
Yet like most Vermonters,
I speak plainly,
and greet passersby
with a casual wave.
My life is stitched plain but true.

I write to understand–
to stumble and rise,
to unearth small truths,
and welcome whoever
chooses to join.